Francesca Filosa

essays by

Laura Andreini
Luca Molinari
Luca Orlandi
Alper Derinboğaz

ON THE ROAD city
Istanbul

ON THE ROAD
Editor of collection
Laura Andreini

editorial project
Forma Edizioni srl, Florence, Italy
redazione@formaedizioni.it
www.formaedizioni.it

editorial production
Archea Associati

editorial direction
Laura Andreini

author
Francesca Filosa*

editorial staff
Maria Giulia Caliri
Livia D'Aliasi
Giulia Di Stefano
Monica Giannini

graphic design
Silvia Agozzino
Isabella Peruzzi
Veronica Paoli

translations
Katy Hannan

First Edition: May 2024

ISBN 978-88-55210-84-3

texts by
Laura Andreini
Luca Molinari
Luca Orlandi
Alper Derinboğaz

Francesca Filosa: pp. 30-40, 44-54, 58, 60, 64-72, 78, 82-88, 94-104, 110, 114- 118, 124, 128, 130, 136, 138, 142, 146, 152-162, 166, 170, 176, 184-196, 202
Alessandro Virgilio Mosetti: pp. 42, 56, 74, 76, 80, 90, 92, 112, 120, 122, 126, 132, 134, 140, 164, 168, 172, 174, 180, 182, 198, 200

* **Francesca Filosa**, is an independent researcher and architect, and holds a PhD in Architecture, Theory and Project Design from the Università La Sapienza di Roma with a doctoral dissertation entitled *Spazi Mostruosi: per un'architettura trans-specie*. She has written scientific articles for specialised magazines and has spoken at various conferences where she analyses the relationship between constructed spaces and non-human animals. She currently has a private practice, conducting research and work on antispeciesist architecture.

Table of contents

Guidebook as a Tool

On the Road is a collection of contemporary architecture guidebooks whose purpose is to tell about a place, whether a city or larger area, through its architectural works chosen to be visited and experienced directly.

The guidebook has a convenient special jacket that opens into a map marking the location of the architectural works and interesting sites to visit. On the back are miniature images and addresses of the architectural works described in detail within.

The book starts with short essays explaining the city or area's present day and history and outlining possible future scenarios with planned or imminent projects. Each work features a photograph of the whole, an architectural drawing (plan or section), a short description, and facts including architect, type, year of construction, address, website, and how to visit it.

The finest architecture of each city and suggested routes are represented by this collection of not-to-be-missed, "timeless" buildings that uniquely define their settings. General information and useful tips for travelers help them optimize their visits and quickly understand the essence of the place described.

Museums, theatres, restaurants, hotels and a list of top architectural firms working in the city let visitors turn a regular trip into an opportunity for study or work.

Note: The pinpoints outside the maps at the beginning of the itineraries are viewable on the rear of the book jacket.

Istanbul

Laura Andreini*

In his introduction to *Costantinopoli*, the book written by Edmondo De Amicis and republished by Einaudi in 2007, Umberto Eco referred to Istanbul as "Una e Trina", [a Trinity of three cultures] describing it as a fascinating city of myths and legends, to be discovered little by little, wandering its winding streets, free to gaze and absorb the city's endless diversity.

While researching this book dedicated to Istanbul for the On the Road series, as we strolled through the streets of this metropolis, we too realised that it represented a journey in space and time, through a myriad of different periods and civilisations. To gain a true reading of this place, one must explore the multiple layers accumulated over the centuries and which continue to be generated at the present time, determined by an intricate weave of both conservation and modernisation.

The exploration of Istanbul is divided into five itineraries; each one reveals the huge complexity of this capital which coexists with its numerous identities. A long journey that begins in the historic centre, home to the majestic Basilica of Hagia Sofia, symbol of the city and its Byzantine architecture, moving on towards Beyoğlu, a district with a strong European influence, rich in museums and art galleries. Here, the Istanbul Modern by Renzo Piano sits alongside monumental buildings from the Ottoman period, like the 16th century Kılıç Ali Paşa mosque by Sinan, the Baroque Nusretiye mosque, the Tophane Kasrı summer palace, and the Tophane-i Amire canon foundry; an excessive urban accumulation where contemporary architecture contrasts with that of ancient civilisations, a characteristic that increases as one moves further north towards the districts of Beşiktaş and Şişli.

The European part of the city flows on to the districts of Kağıthane, Beşiktaş, Sarıyer and Eyüp with some of Istanbul's most important infrastructures: the Fatih Sultan Mehmet Köprüsü and Yavuz Sultan Selim bridges, true examples of avant-garde engineering, that connect the European and Asian sides of the city.

This finally leads to the other shore of the Bosporus, in particular, the districts of Kadiköy, Üsküar and Ataşehir, areas of the city under vast expansion, dense with contemporary architecture, where even the religious buildings are in contrast with the mosques in the historic centre.

In this guide, we take the opportunity to pay homage to the complex territories which define a city that straddles two continents, which has been a melting pot of different cultures, religions, and aesthetics for centuries.

We hope the suggested itineraries will act as inspiration, but also as an invitation to roam the streets of a city that, over the course of its history, has changed its name from Byzantium to Constantinople, to the present day Istanbul, without ever ceasing "to remain the same".

* Laura Andreini is Architect and Associate Professor at DIDA, University of Florence. Co-founder of Studio Archea where she still works, she is also writer and deputy editor for *area* magazine.

Political / geographical facts

country
Turkey

language
turkish

area code
+90 21

coordinates
41°01'N
28°58'E

area
5,343 sq. km

population
15,569 856

density
3,748.69 inhabitants / sq.km

time zone
UTC+2

city website
www.ibb.istanbul

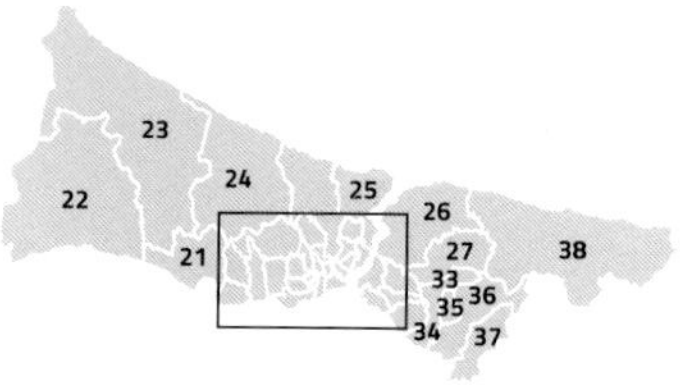

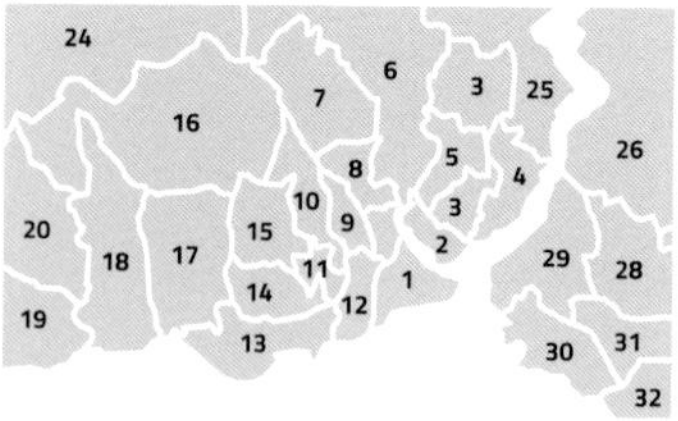

Administrative districts

1. Fatih
2. Beyoğlu
3. Şişli
4. Beşiktaş
5. Kağithane
6. Eyüpsultan
7. Sultangazi
8. Gaziosmanpaşa
9. Esenler
10. Bayrampaşa
11. Güngören
12. Zeytinburnu
13. Bakırköy
14. Bahçelievler
15. Bağcilar
16. Başakşehir
17. Küçükçekmece
18. Avcılar
19. Beylikdüzü
20. Esenyurt
21. Büyükçekmece
22. Silivri
23. Çatalca
24. Arnavutköy
25. Sarıyer
26. Beykoz
27. Çekmeköy
28. Ümraniye
29. Üsküdar
30. Kadıköy
31. Ataşehir
32. Maltepe
33. Sancaktepe
34. Kartal
35. Sultanbeyli
36. Pendik
37. Tuzla
38. Şile

General information
useful addresses and numbers

INFORMATION OFFICES

Instabul Touristic Office
General Direction of Suleyman
Seba Cad., No: 7,
34357 Beșiktaș, Istanbul
(+90) (212) 2587760

EMERGENCY SERVICES

Police 155
Touristic Police (+90) (212) 527 45 03
Vigili del fuoco 110
Emergency medical service 112
General Emergencies 112
Touristic Information 170

URBAN TRANSPORT

The site www.iett.istanbul provides useful information on all means of transport available in the city, how to buy tickets, and ordinary and season ticket fares.

Taxi
Flughafen Taxi: (+90) (212) 237 49 95
Pera Taxi: (+90) (212) 243 83 99
Fat Taxi: (+90) (532) 662 21 45
Taxis can also be booked online at www.booktaxiistanbul.com or using the BiTaksi App downloadable from App Store or Google Play

Bicycle rentals
Instanbul on Bike
Bicycles and bike tours can also be booked online at www.istanbulonbike.com

Car sharing
Yolcu360, Rentiva, Garajyeri, Rent Go, Otokoc Otomotiv, Otoendeks

EMBASSY OF ITALY
Tom Tom Kaptan Sokak, 5
34433 Beyoğlu, Istanbul
(+90) (212) 243 10 24/5, 252 54 37, 251 32 94

GENERAL CONSULATE OF FRANCE
Istiklal Caddesi, 4
Taksim 34435, Istanbul
(+90) (212) 334 87 30

GENERAL CONSULATE OF GERMANY
Inono Caddesi, 10
34437 Gemessuyu, PK 6,
34431 Beyoğlu, Istanbul
(+90) (212) 334 61 00

EMBASSY OF THE UNITED STATES
Poligon Mahallesi, Sariyer Caddesi, 75
İstinye 34460 Sariyer, Istanbul
(+90) (212) 335 90 00

ITALIAN CONSOLATE GENERAL
Tom Tom Kaptan Sokak, 5
(+90) (212) 243 10 24

HOW TO PHONE

From a local landline: Just dial the number, including the city code (0)212

From a foreign landline: Dial the international code (+90), city code (212) and number

Useful tips

1. Istanbul offers a wide range of accommodation from low cost to medium-high prices, able to satisfy the needs of all types of tourist and budget. The Fatih district and the Sultanahmet quarter are home to some of the most elegant luxury hotels like the **Hotel Arcadia Blue Istanbul**, the **Four Seasons Hotel Istanbul** at **Sultanahmet** and the **Ajwa Hotel Sultanahmet**, which offer panoramic views of Hagia Sofia and the Blue Mosque. Along the banks of the Bosphorus, there are very good hotels including the **Çırağan Palace Kempinski Istanbul**. For less expensive accommodation, Istanbul has a vast choice of reasonably priced B&Bs, especially in the Beyoğlu district, where there are excellent solutions with good value for money.

2. Public transport is efficient and provides convenient access to all areas of the city. Travel options include the **metropolitan** (subway), the **funicular** (cable car) and **tram service**, which close at midnight. However, all the main **bus lines** run 24 hours a day. Public transport may seem a little complicated at first, but with a little practice and a smartphone app, it is much easier. One way to fully enjoy the city is to travel on foot: the principal areas, especially in the historic centre, are full of narrow winding streets, where visitors can enjoy the unique atmosphere and close-up views of the buildings that make up this fascinating city.

3. The **ferry** is one of the most frequent means of transport to travel between the eastern and western sides of the city. Seeing Istanbul from the water is undoubtedly one of the most delightful experiences. Short cruises along the Bosphorus are also available and highly recommended, as crossing the straits provides wonderful views of the skyline. This form of transport is not simply a tourist attraction but is a common means for local inhabitants who can admire the beauty of the city reflected in the waters of the Bosphorus.

4. Istanbul is deservedly famous for its **mosques** and **monuments**, which give the city a unique and exclusive atmosphere. Among the most beautiful are the historic mosques like the **Hagia Sofia** (Ayasofya Camii), the **Blue Mosque**, (Sultan Ahemet Camii), the **Suleiman Mosque** (Süleymaniye Camii), the New Mosque (Yeni Cami), the **Eyüp Sultan Mosque**, and the elegant contemporary architecture of the **Yeşilvadi Mosque** and the **Sancaklar Mosque**. Istanbul is also home to a large number of **museums** and **theatres** which attract considerable crowds every year. Not to be missed is a visit to the historic museums like the **Topkapı Palace** and the modern galleries such as the **Istanbul Modern** and the **Deniz Müzesi** on the banks of the Bosphorus, which house collections of modern art, but also narrate the history of the city. Other interesting buildings worth visiting are the restoration and expansion projects on historic buildings like the **Pera Müzesi**, the **IKSV** and the **SALT Galata**, which are fascinating not only for their architectural interest but for their extremely important cultural and social relevance, where visitors can admire works of art and participate in cultural events.

5. There is virtually nothing you cannot find in the Istanbul markets. One of the largest is **Kapali Çarşi**, the vast covered market, one of the oldest and most fascinating, a city within a city. The **Kadıköy Çarşısı** is where to go for spices and aromatic herbs, an endless range of aromas and colours to delight the senses. For antique books, miniature paintings and art books, visit the **Sahaflar Çarşısı**, the historic bazaar in Fatih. The **Beşiktaş Balık Pazarı** is the renowned fish market that not only offers a vast selection of food products, but is also famous for being an important attraction in Beşiktaş, because of its avant garde design and contemporary architecture. On the Asian side of the city, one of the most famous markets is the **Leman Kültür Kadıköy** an excellent food market renowned for its traditional coffee pots and local shops selling authentic Ottoman confectionery.

6. Inside the markets you will find a vast selection of tasty **street foods** with Turkish specialities like *simit, kokoreç, pilav* and *midiye*. If you want to relax and sit down for a meal, there are many small eateries around Beşiktaş Balık Pazarı, somewhat spartan, some on stilt houses, but with excellent food full of flavour, spices and aromas. They also have great views of the old city. Turkish cuisine is one of the most renowned, complex, and varied in the world because of Istanbul's rich history as a melting pot of so many nationalities, and as a consequence, the food has been influenced and enriched by a range of different cultures. The **Meyhane** are traditional taverns that sell alcoholic drinks, while there is a vast range of local restaurants for every taste and budget.

7. Istanbul is rich in green parks and public squares carved out of the dense urban fabric. Some of the most famous historic parks are **Gülhane Parkı**, in the Fatih district, the **Yıldız Parkı**, one of the largest in the city, and **Emirgan Korusu**. These are delightful spaces to relax and enjoy nature, away from the frenetic chaos of the city.

Istanbul, an Architectural Worksite Between Modernity and Tradition

Luca Molinari*

The maps and infographics in the impressive publication, *Mapping Istanbul*, edited in 2009 by Pelin Dervis and Meric Oner, provide an immediate idea of the turbulent expansion of what is now the most densely populated metropolis in Europe with a population of about 16 million inhabitants.

The taxi ride to the city centre from the two airports on the extreme Asian and European margins of the city, gives a first-hand perception of the enormous size of the metropolitan area and the new infrastructures that are creating constant expansion. Also visible is the widespread construction of the large residential settlements necessary to house the rapidly increasing population.

Like many other huge cities, contemporary Istanbul can be read as a complex archipelago composed of almost autonomous islands that have followed the evolution of the city's growth through the centuries, to finally explode in recent decades.

Byzantium/Constantinople/Stambul/Istanbul has always been a global centre because of its political, cultural, economic and social importance. The relationship between the form and geography of the city conditioned the morphology and settlement patterns. Initially the population was forced to live within the walls that protected the Roman, Byzantine and Ottoman capitals, but later the population expanded, above all along the Asian side.

The true problem lies in the present expansion since there has been a decline in the original architectural style, an image of the city, in the name of a generic and globalised condition, partly as the result of real estate capital pressure, but also a public and private clientele increasingly less aware of the character of Istanbul.

The relationship with the idea of modernity led to a very interesting evolution between the 19th and 20th centuries, above all thanks to the presence of German, French and Italian architects and engineers, initially called by the last Pashas to give the ancient capital a modern European aspect. But the fashionable western models gradually became assimilated by a cosmopolitan cultural and social context accustomed to comparison with the stylistic influences that arrived from west to east of the Empire.

Another interesting element was the fortunate encounter between a tectonic idea of civil and monumental architecture, emblematic of Ottoman culture, through several generations of designers beginning with Sinān, and the rationalist austerity of the first designers experimenting with reinforced concrete. They were inspired by the direct influence and teachings of Perret, as well as the more traditionalist modernism based on the Teutonic matrix of Paul Bonatz and Clemenz Holzmeister. In this professional world and with technical education, the first generations of Turkish Modernist architects followed these cultural models and merged with a careful reading of the historical and monumental heritage of the Ottoman Renaissance.

It is only in this way we can understand the strength and influence of

* Luca Molinari is a full Professor of Architectural Design at Campania University and writes as an independent author for various Italian and international publications. Alongside his work in academics and research, he also works as a curator and writer.

Sedad Hakki Eldem, the undisputed master of modern architecture in Istanbul, whose style became the image of a modem republican state, secular and close to Europe, without being passively subject to its influences. A series of public buildings like the Faculty of Science and Letters designed by Eldem define the character of a Turkish Modernist monumental style that marked a whole generation of public architecture, almost in contrast with the International Style of the Hilton Hotel, created in 1948 by the American firm, SOM, on the edge of the historical centre, and which became synonymous with another more globalised trend that was to mark a current of contemporary Turkish architecture.

At the end of the Second World War, and despite the country's persistent political fragility, modern architecture defined the collective imagination of a metropolis that was no longer the capital of Turkey, but remained its economic and cultural heart.

From that moment, there were two recognisable currents that moved along parallel and often mutually tangential lines; one line sought recourse in the secular and conscious relationship with Ottoman tradition with which it could communicate freely, and the second followed a globalised and updated vision of international dialogue.

Turkish architectural culture has always demonstrated a strong dialogue with stylistic phenomena across the world, but always tempered by a strongly conscious and rarely reactionary nationalistic sense which has been able to assimilate pressure, even the most extreme.

Today this situation is very well represented on one hand by the work of Han Tümertekin who in the last two decades has reached a level of maturity that puts him on the same level as many foreign colleagues thanks to projects like the restoration of the SALT Galata building, or the city's National Library with the restoration of an ancient Ottoman military barracks. On the other hand, it is more fragmented thanks to the presence of two equally talented architectural firms, Tabanlıoğlu Architects and Emre Arolat, followed by the next generation, with projects on a lesser scale designed by Alper Derinbogaz/Salon architects, GAD, Superpool and MarS-Architects, who demonstrate a more updated dialogue and more experimental trends gathered from the contemporary scene.

This research work struggles to establish itself within turbulent and disorganised expansion; on one hand, the existing historical heritage which deserves greater public attention, and on the other, the glutinous treacle of generic building schemes that invade the new residential suburbs and business centre with complete indifference. This contrast is totally unbalanced if we are to hope in a different future, but I am certain that environmental and water emergencies could become a crucial aspect that even Istanbul will have to deal with to find alternative solutions for controlling its expansion in the decades to come.

Forgetting and Rethinking Istanbul

Luca Orlandi*

Almost 90 years ago, the travel writer and aesthete, Robert Byron, wrote that there are certain cases when the beauty of urban landscapes and architecture elude the analysis of human thought and judgement and transcend the objectives of critical generalisation. The city of Constantinople/Istanbul belongs to this category, emerging – in his words – "like a mirage in the midst of the Sea of Marmara".

With its almost 16 million inhabitants and area of about 5,400 square kilometres, today, the city of Istanbul is one of the most crowded megalopolises in the world, constantly growing with a kind of urban bulimia that seems to suppress and erase its magnificent past. It is hard to say what remains of Byron's "mirage" today. The first thing seen by those who arrive by sea is the bleak skyline of very modern towering skyscrapers that dominate and overshadow almost every district in the city. Travellers today would find it hard to be stirred by Byron's ecstatic reflections on the architecture and urban landscapes of the "Capital" of the Orient.

However, it is pointless to compare Istanbul with other megacities that exist in Eurasia, the African continent, or in the two Americas, since no other city in the world has been the capital of three empires, and no other city physically sits astride two continents in a precarious balance between opposing but complementary cultures like those of the Occident and the Orient.

For thousands of years it has been the centre, port and crossroads of different civilisations and religious faiths, eternally suspended between Asia and Europe: Istanbul can be defined as a contemporary ancient metropolis in constant evolution, with its multiple and often contradictory identities, its constant process of assimilation, conservation, destruction, and renewal; it could almost be defined as fluid rather than terrestrial, in some ways glutinous, like the language of the city's inhabitants.

In this period of global and globalising dynamics, the problem of the rational development of a contemporary city in the midst of reckless and greedy markets is not limited only and exclusively to the Turkish metropolis. However, perhaps because of its thousands of years of history, its role as a capital city in ancient times, and its fluctuating geopolitical and territorial existence in constant search of equilibrium, today Istanbul appears like a city that is in danger of losing its identity, between a past of unimaginable splendour and a present (and future?) of tangible uncertainty.

Like the melancholic and despondent novels of Orhan Pamuk, Istanbul's streets, quarters and new business districts, the huge infrastructures that cross the city, the housing density of its suburbs, and exponential growth of its population, constantly portray all these contradictions; however, the solutions proposed to try and contain these phenomena caused by an irrational and deregulated globalisation, do not always seem possible.

Istanbul's rapid development and aggressive entry among the 21st century

* Luca Orlandi is an Architectural Historian who has lived and worked in Istanbul for almost 20 years, where he teaches Architectural History and Architectural Design at Özyeğin University.
He is a member of the international associations, ICOMOS and EAHN.

global megacities coincided with the arrival on the political scene of the new Justice and Development Party (Adalet ve Kalkınma Partisi or AKP), a moderate conservative Islamic party that won the elections in 2002 and that has governed the country ever since, despite the unfortunate political and social events of recent years. The idea of building a New Turkey, or Yeni Turkiye, according to the party's propaganda language, completely detached from its recent republican past, is one of the main objectives on the agenda, through reforms that mainly affect urban planning and architecture. Reforms and projects that are planned for completion before 2023, the 100th anniversary of the Turkish Republic.

However, as far as protecting and preserving the historical-architectural legacy of Istanbul is concerned, more than in other cities, there is a general problem where the authorities in charge do not seem (or want) to seek adequate solutions. There are many situations where vulnerable heritage sites are ignored, or are dealt with in a hasty and often superficial way, without suitably predicting the consequences, and this contributes towards irreparable damage to the historic patrimony.

More because of political policy and government strategy than through objective needs for restoration, in recent years, the trend has been to prioritise interventions aimed at improving everything linked with the post 1453 era, in other words, the historic period that relates exclusively to the Turkish-Ottoman culture, neglecting both the previous ancient history, and the more recent republican past, and in these cases, often with mediocre results.

In many areas of the city, rich in artistic and architectural heritage of certain historical and cultural importance, planning decisions linked with conservation are often not aimed at a true protection of historic buildings, but simply become window dressing operations, where the monument becomes a stage set, more or less authentic, like a theme park, where cultural aspects are used only for entertainment. There are endless examples of this practice and several cases are included here as examples.

The subway bridge, completed in 2014, that crosses the Golden Horn, connecting the Historical Peninsular with the European zone of Beyoğlu, is undoubtedly one of the most controversial projects of the past 10 years. In order to build this important infrastructure, it was considered preferable to sacrifice the remains of the 14th century walls of the Genoese colony in Galata. For seven years, the authorities have been absolutely indifferent to the fact that a visual and tangible trace of the city's past history has been left abandoned and neglected. A similar situation occurred with the hub-station of Yenikapı, in the Historical Peninsular, following an international competition aimed at focusing attention on the archaeological park linked with the ancient port that was discovered during the excavations for the subway tunnel and ferry boat access. Unfortunately, adequate upgrade solutions were not proposed during the competition and for this reason the archaeological site was not integrated within the project. It exists simply as an empty urban space "with visible ruins", that cannot be used by the public, and that are almost unidentifiable as the remains of the millenary Byzantine past of the city.

However, even in the case of large restoration projects, such as the Süleymaniye Mosque, built during the most magnificent period of Ottoman art, one would expect to see greater attention paid to the renovation work, given the emphasis placed by the current government on promoting and enhancing its Ottoman heritage. And yet, the hasty restorations carried out for the Istanbul European Capital of Culture in 2010, demonstrated an incapacity to manage large-scale sites where the main objective seemed only to conclude the restoration in time, within the established date, but without taking into consideration the complexity and problems connected with buildings of this kind.

There are other similar examples, but it would seem that, for a city like Istanbul, with its stratigraphy, and the complex transformations that have changed the morphology of the city over the centuries, the common denominator should surely be "to remember so as not to forget", by connecting the past and present. This should be one of the basic requirements for the correct conservation of this extremely rich heritage. Often, in line with the reasoning of partisan interests, many financial investments, sustained by both public and private sectors, are used for restoration and renovation interventions in historic areas; however they often forget that these are exceptional urban environments, and consider only the present without any concern for the future.

In its recent history, Istanbul has demonstrated that it is a vibrant, alert international city, interested in new trends, rich in cultural events, able to attract tourists and investors from other countries. Its entire history deserves to be recognised, without giving precedence to specific periods while ignoring others. Perhaps it deserves to be an aesthetic rather than an ecstatic mirage once again for the new Byrons of the 21st century. The multicultural legacy and diversity of its millenary architectural heritage should be reconsidered as a treasure and an added value to be handed down for posterity in a conscious manner, not simply as sporadic opportunities for speculation and financial transactions, or even worse, for ideological expediency.

Geo Cryptic

Alper Derinboğaz*

Despite the massive amount of new housing and techno-conservative government projects, contemporary Istanbul is still a charming and liberating city. James Baldwin "felt freedom in the streets", and Edmondo De Amicis found the city the most beautiful place on earth. But where does this charm originate? I believe every architect will enjoy discovering this for themselves. However, there are some fundamental aspects in this city that could help to lay the foundations for personal interpretation.

* Alper Derinboğaz graduated from the Technical University of Istanbul. He is a founding partner of Salon Architects, directs an architectural design firm, and seminars on "Media Architecture" at Bilgi University of Istanbul.

Geographical Self Planning

For many reasons, I think that most metropolises did not develop in extreme geographical sites. This does not apply to Istanbul, perhaps because the dramatic topography is an integral part of the city's unique and strategic defensive position on the Bosphorus strait. Unquestionably the picturesque quality of the city's geographical diversity has always charmed painters, poets and writers.

Beyond its panoramic beauty, Istanbul presents challenges for urban designers, transportation engineers and architects, because of its site as the only transcontinental city in the world. Until now the geography has always had a stronger influence than urban planning or governmental decisions on the development and form of the city. An example of this is the designated "Finance Center" in Ataşehir. This grandiose project with vast institutional investments and governmental incentives is now called the "bottomless pit" despite all the efforts invested. Meanwhile, Büyükdere Avenue was developed without urban planning and has simply continued to grow with soaring rents and real estate value.

The city did not develop with any kind of order as we know it because the city expansion focussed on the infrastructure, following the valleys and concentrating on the ridges. We can follow the Büyükdere ridge on the European Side, beginning from the Galata Tower up to the Tunnel Square, extending from Taksim Square to Şişli, from Zincirlikuyu to Levent, and from the 4. Levent Station to Maslak. Travelling along the ridge is almost like following a timeline in a history book, moving the financial centre step by step from Galata up to Maslak.

In 1937, Henri Prost, a French architect and urban planner, designed and proposed a central green belt starting from Maçka Valley through to Gezi Park, and then as far as Taksim Square. The green belt was largely completed, but it did not survive as the first Hilton Hotel by SOM divided a very critical portion of the green corridor. Dismantling continued with other commercial projects until another incentive was planned to demolish the last portion of this central green space. In 2013 Istanbul witnessed one of the largest protest movements as a result of an urban development proposal. Despite the removal of a large percentage of green space over the years, the Gezi Park protests represent an important achievement in terms of public participation in urban decisions and the protection of green space, resulting in setting up neighbourhood forums in search of direct democracy.

Small is Big

Local citizens often felt threatened by mega projects such as Galataport, Zorlu Center, Four Winds or Cevahir Shopping Center. I believe the main reason is because they eat away at publicly-owned lands. These large-scale commercial projects easily get out of hand, mainly because of ambiguous building permits, poor public engagement, disproportionately large structures, and the lack of contribution to public life.

Despite its large scale, the city still has many minor beauties. In the labyrinthic intricacy of the smaller streets one can allow oneself to get lost, in an era when getting lost is rare. Strolling around the streets of Cihangir provides a great chance to see beautiful examples of art deco houses with panoramic views of the Bosphorus, built for the middle classes. The Princes' Islands and Moda, "Adalar, Modalar", are generally considered some of the more exclusive residential districts in the city, showcasing many refined modernistic structures from apartment buildings to clubhouses and pools. In addition to architecture-led projects the majority of the constructions are apartments with about 20 years of life expectancy and a rapid flexibility that metabolists could envy.

Florya Atatürk Marine Mansion (1935) designed by architect Seyfi Arkan is an avant-garde building embracing the Republic's enlightened vision. Alfred Heilbronn's Botanic Garden in the Historic Peninsula, dating to 1934, is again an interesting late modern structure bringing history, nature and science together in a unique way.

Emerging Contemporary Culture Core

An impressive competition was launched among various corporations following the construction of the Istanbul Modern Museum, founded by Eczacıbaşı in 2003. Later, as part of the Bilgi University Santral Istanbul master plan, a contemporary art museum was built, although it ended as a half-realised dream as the foundation was privatized. A series of new buildings followed, shaping their trajectories with other institutions such as the SALT, Sabancı Museum, Borusan Contemporary, Arter, Meşher, Pera Museum and Yapı Kredi Museum. These contemporary buildings led to restoring interest in Beyoglu, which had long been an important centre in the heart of the city and is testament to the radical changes that have affected the city centre. I believe these buildings are important contributions, setting examples for ways to recover, restore, refine and advance what exists in a city that tends to forget its past.

As well as the private institutions, while not forgetting the impressive, army-funded Naval Museum, the Istanbul City Museum will be the first publicly-owned new museum in Istanbul. The struggle for a city museum for Istanbul dates back to 1996, and in 2015 following the exhibition of *Modalities of Spontaneous* at the Venice Biennale, our architectural firm was assigned the role of project architects. Besides the meticulous exhibition curated by Luca Molinari, the building is planned as a centre for cultural activities together with the park and Byzantine Walls, forming a new cultural axis around the historic peninsula.

Following all the ambiguous planning regulations, historic fires and disruptive commercial projects, Istanbul is a completely unpredictable, surprising and chaotic city that could be defined as geo cryptic because of its unique transcontinental geography. Because Istanbul still conserves the memory of its geographic genetics.

Blue Mosque
(Sultan Ahemet Camii)
Istanbul Erkek
PTT – Grand Post Office
Istanbul Ticaret odasi

Süleymaniye Mosque
(Süleymaniye Camii)
Germanya Han
Yeni Camii
Hünkar Kasrı
Galata Bridge

Fraser Place Anthill Istanbul
Hilton Istanbul Bomonti Hotel & Conference Center
Atatürk Bridge
Haliç Altın Boynuz

Bomonti Plaza
Sokullu Mehmet Pasha Mosque
İBB Karaköy Sahil Parkı

Strategies for visiting Istanbul

Visiting Istanbul means exploring the culture and the wonders of an ancient people, and we recommend at least a week in order to gain a true insight into the city. This guide proposes five itineraries and offers a wide coverage of the city's architectural heritage, with mainly contemporary design as well as buildings of historical/artistic interest. The itineraries cover every zone in the city and can all be reached by public transport as indicated.

Itinerary A | Fatih
The first route travels through the historic heart of the city. Symbolically, to fully understand and explore Istanbul, tours begin with **Hagia Sophia Grand Mosque/01** [Ayasofya Camii], whose majestic architecture and breathtaking internal mosaics immediately plunge the visitor into some of the most iconic and prodigious architecture in Istanbul. The **Grand Bazaar of Istanbul/03** [Kapalı Çarşı], government and administration buildings, the Roman **Aqueduct of Valens/09** [Valens Su Kemeri], and the **Topkapı Palace/13** [Topkapı Sarayı], bear witness to the amazing historical and artistic treasures of the city.

Itinerary B | Beyoğlu
The Beyoğlu area enables visitors to explore some of the museums and cultural centres that play a very important role in the community, including **SALT Galata/17**, **Suma Han/19**, **IKSV – İstanbul Kültür Sanat Vakfi/36** [Istanbul Foundation for Culture and Arts], **Borusan Art/30** [Borusan Sanat], **2F Evi/20**, **Zemin Istanbul/34**, **Garaj İstanbul/27**, and **The Museum of Innocence/26** [Masumiyet Müzesi]: the famous literary museum born from the pen of Nobel Prize Winner, Orhan Pamuk. Inside the Beyoğlu quarter is **Şışhane Park/35**, one of Istanbul's contemporary public spaces, carved out from a junction of busy roads in a residential area. This route also allows the visitor to compare cutting edge experiments in modern residential architecture such as **Ipera 25/21** and **NoXX Apartment/25**, where contemporary design is proposed in contrast with traditional Turkish housing like the early 20th century buildings by the architect, Raimondo D'Aronco.

Itinerary C | Beşiktaş - Şişli
The Beşiktaş – Şişli route covers quite a large area to the north of the city. It houses a number of modern and contemporary buildings. In the Beşiktaş district is the **Fish market/53** [Beşiktaş Balık Pazarı] a contemporary design that remodelled and created a new space for the traditional open air market for direct food sale to the public. Further along the route on the Bosphorus coast is the famous **Istanbul Naval Museum/52** [Deniz Müzesi], that houses the remains of ancient ships and other objects belonging to the city's maritime history. The route also leads to the **July 15th Martyrs**

Bridge/56 [15 temmuz şehitler köprüsü], known as Bosphorus bridge. Just above it, clinging to the hillside, is **Taut House/55** [Taut Evi] designed by the expressionist architect, Bruno Taut.

Itinerary D | Kadiköy - Üsküar - Ataşehir

The Asian side of Istanbul mainly houses the financial district and business centre showing the huge recent development, with contemporary architecture that is symbolic of an economically competitive major city. Once again, traditional architecture is re-proposed with state of the art contemporary design and aesthetics. An excellent example is the **Yeşilvadi Mosque/68** [Yeşilvadi Camii], a curving, circular, domed building that reinterprets elements of traditional mosque design. Another quarter well worth visiting is **Fashion Headquarters/57** [Vakko Moda Merkezi] located in the lively Kadiköy district, well-known for its picturesque narrow streets, shops, boutiques, cafes, and restaurants.

Itinerary E | Kağıthane - Beşiktaş - Sarıyer - Eyüp

The Kağıthane - Beşiktaş - Sarıyer - Eyüp area contains a number of interesting buildings which, although not close to one another, can be easily reached by bus or the Metro. This route includes the **Fatih Sultan Mehmet/70** [Fatih Sultan Mehmet Köprüsü] and **Yavuz Sultan Selim bridges/72** which are true feats of avant-garde engineering, and represent the extremely significant link between the European and Asian sides of Istanbul. This itinerary also includes the **Istanbul Grand Airport/74** designed by the London firm, Grimshaw Architects, and the **Santralistanbul/78**, an important redevelopment intervention with the conversion of a former electrical power plant into a museum and cultural centre. This area of the city is also home to the **Sancaklar Mosque/75** [Sancaklar Camii], a modern interpretation of the traditional mosque, and an example of contemporary design that should not be missed by architecture lovers.

Routes

A. Fatih
B. Beyoğlu
C. Beşiktaş - Şişli
D. Kadıköy - Üsküar - Ataşehir
E. Kağıthane - Beşiktaş - Sarıyer - Eyüp

E
C1
C2
B
A2
A1
D1
D2

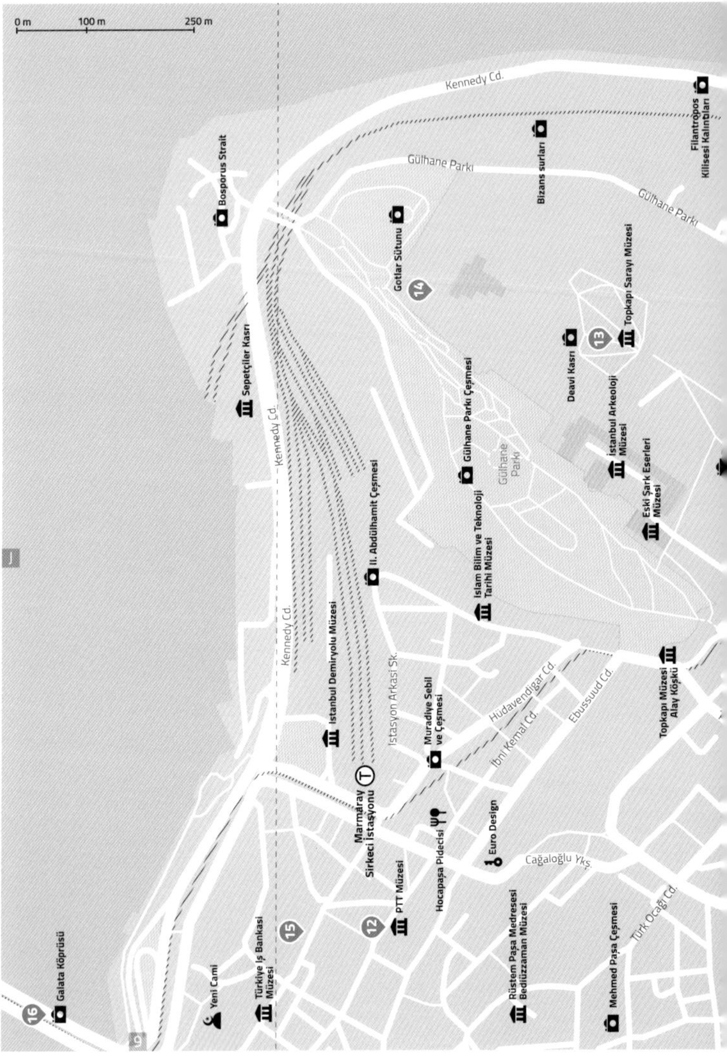
0 m
100 m
250 m
Kennedy Cd.
Bosporus Strait
Gülhane Parkı
Bizans surları
Filantropos Kilisesi Kalıntıları
Gotlar Sütunu
14
Topkapı Sarayı Müzesi
13
Deavi Kasrı
Sepetçiler Kasrı
Gülhane Parkı Çeşmesi
Gülhane Parkı
İstanbul Arkeoloji Müzesi
Eski Şark Eserleri Müzesi
II. Abdülhamit Çeşmesi
Islam Bilim ve Teknoloji Tarihi Müzesi
İstanbul Demiryolu Müzesi
İstasyon Arkası Sk.
Muradiye Sebil ve Çeşmesi
Hüdavendigar Cd.
İbni Kemal Cd.
Ebussuud Cd.
Topkapı Müzesi Alay Köşkü
Marmaray Sirkeci İstasyonu
Hocapaşa Pidecisi
Euro Design
Cağaloğlu Ykş.
PTT Müzesi
12
15
Rüstem Paşa Medresesi Bediüzzaman Müzesi
Mehmed Paşa Çeşmesi
Türk Ocağı Cd.
Türkiye İş Bankası Müzesi
Yeni Cami
Galata Köprüsü
16
J
G

Fatih

01. Hagia Sophia Grand Mosque
02. Ayasofya Hürrem Sultan Hamamı
03. Grand Bazaar of Istanbul
04. Beyazıt State Library
05. Istanbul University Observatory
06. Istanbul University Faculty of Literature
07. Istanbul Metropolitan Municipality building

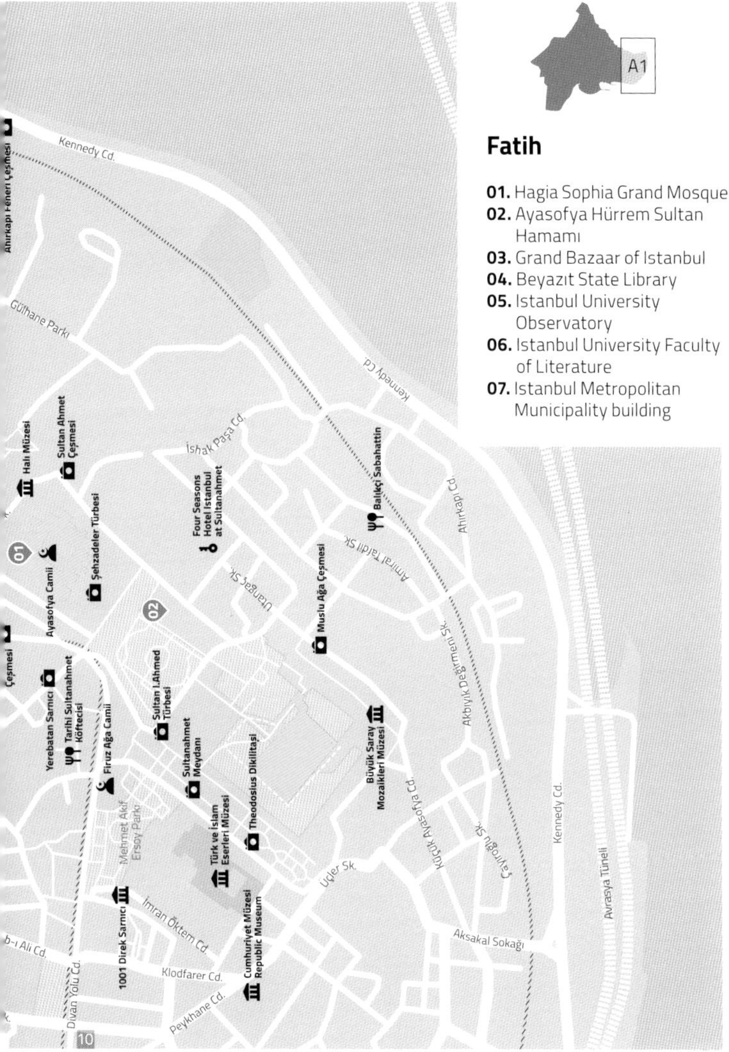

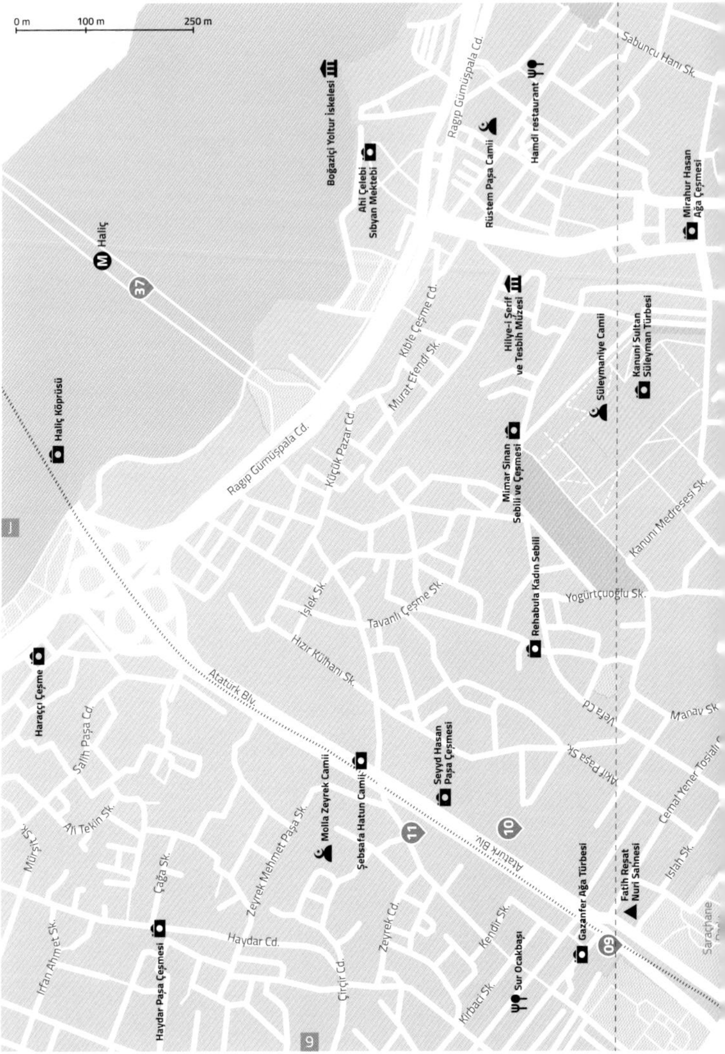

0 m
100 m
250 m
Boğaziçi Yoltur İskelesi
Haliç
37
Haliç Köprüsü
Ahi Çelebi Sıbyan Mektebi
Ragıp Gümüşpala Cd.
Rüstem Paşa Camii
Hamdi restaurant
Sabuncu Hanı Sk.
Mirahur Hasan Ağa Çeşmesi
Hilye-i Şerif ve Tesbih Müzesi
Kıble Çeşme Cd.
Murat Efendi Sk.
Küçük Pazar Cd.
Süleymaniye Camii
Kanuni Sultan Süleyman Türbesi
Mimar Sinan Sebili ve Çeşmesi
Kanuni Medresesi Sk.
Rehabula Kadın Sebili
Yoğurtçuoğlu Sk.
İşlek Sk.
Tavanlı Çeşme Sk.
Hızır Külhanı Sk.
Atatürk Blv.
Haraççı Çeşme
Salih Paşa Cd.
Vefa Cd.
Manav Sk.
Seyyd Hasan Paşa Çeşmesi
Molla Zeyrek Camii
Şebsafa Hatun Camii
Akif Paşa Sk.
Cemal Yener Tosyalı C.
Ali Tekin Sk.
Mürşit Sk.
Zeyrek Mehmet Paşa Sk.
11
10
Islah Sk.
Çağa Sk.
Zeyrek Cd.
Gazanfer Ağa Türbesi
Fatih Reşat Nuri Sahnesi
Kendir Sk.
09
Saraçhane
İrfan Ahmet Sk.
Haydar Paşa Çeşmesi
Haydar Cd.
Çırçır Cd.
Sur Ocakbaşı
Kırbacı Sk.

Fatih

08. Museum of Istanbul
09. Aqueduct of Valens
10. İMÇ – İstanbul Manifaturacılar Çarşısı
11. Sirkeci Health Center Social Security Supplementary Service Building
12. PTT – Grand Post Office
13. Topkapı Imperial Kitchens
14. Baghdad Kiosk
15. Legacy Ottoman Hotel
16. Galata Bridge

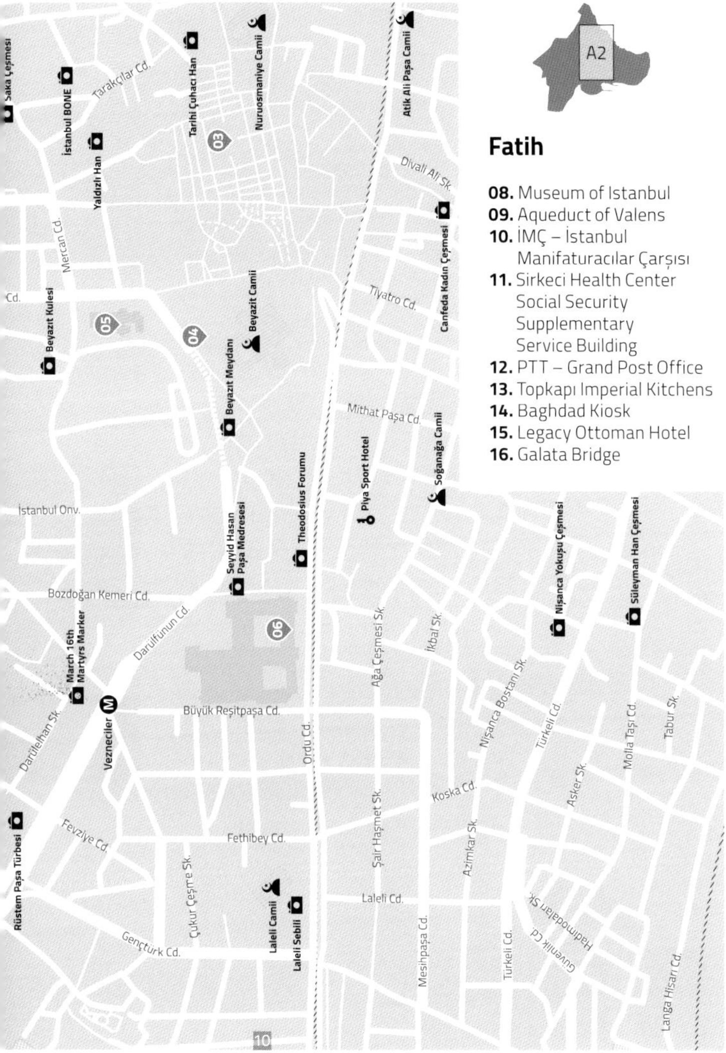

01. Hagia Sophia Grand Mosque

Sultan Ahmet,
Ayasofya Meydanı No:1
34122 Fatih, Istanbul

Tue - Sun / 9 am - 5 pm
+90 212 522 17 50
ayasofyamuzesi.gov.tr/en/contact

B1 > Marmaray Sirkeci

TB2 > Sultanahmet Square
121CS > Sultanahmet
BN1 > Akbıyık

T1 > Sultanahmet

"Glory be to God who judged me worthy of accomplishing this work. Solomon, I have surpassed thee!" These were the words of Emperor Justinian on the completion of the Hagia Sophia Grand Mosque [Ayasofya Camii]. When the building was revealed, it's splendour was magnificent. Built between 532 AD. and 537 AD. the Basilica became the greatest monumental building in the city of Istanbul and was recognised as the triumphant symbol of Byzantine architecture. The project design was assigned to two Greek architects, Isidore of Miletus and Anthemius of Tralles, who combined the central and longitudinal plans to create an elliptical conformation. The internal space is divided into three naves. The central nave is composed of a vast area crowned by a dome, 31 metres in diameter and 55 metres high, flanked by two side half-domes. The base of the central dome is composed of a band with 24 openings that allow light to filter through, creating an evocative glowing circle of light. The light is reflected and diffused by the precious Byzantine mosaics that cover the interior, creating a rare and unique atmosphere. The Basilica was an Eastern Orthodox cathedral until 1453, when it was then converted to a mosque by Mehmed II, and later, the minarets surrounding the monumental dome were added. In 1935, the building was transformed into a museum by Mustafa Kemal Atatürk. In 2020, Turkey's president, Recep Tayyip Erdogan, decided to reintroduce Islamic practice within Santa Sofia, converting the building back to a mosque.

architects
Antemio di Tralle,
Isidoro di Mileto

type
mosque

construction
537

02. Ayasofya Hürrem Sultan Hamamı

Cankurtaran, Ayasofya Meydanı No:2
34122 Fatih, Istanbul

Mon - Sun / 8 am - 10 pm
+90 212 235 90 00
info@ayasofyahamami.com
www.ayasofyahamami.com

B1 > Marmaray Sirkeci

TB2 > Sultanahmet Square
121CS > Sultanahmet
BN1 > Akbıyık

T1 > Sultanahmet

The Hagia Sophia Hurrem Sultan Hammam, located between the Hagia Sophia and the Blue Mosque, was commissioned by Hurrem Sultan, and designed by the architect, Mimar Sinan in 1556. Its revolutionary aspect lies in the distribution layout where, for the first time, the male and female sections were built on the same axis. The structure is 75 metres long and is composed of two bath houses. The internal layouts are symmetrical and the interconnecting rooms follow in sequential order. In the centre of the square changing rooms are a marble fountain and seating benches, surrounded by a magnificent wooden gallery and double staircase. These are connected to the octagonal hot rooms (*sıcaklık*) through two transversal galleries called cool rooms (*soğukluk*). Each section of the complex is roofed with a large lead-covered dome, similar to those found in mosques, recalling the religious significance of ritual bathing. In 2008, the building was restored by the architectural faculty of Kocaeli University which took great care to respect the original design without making any significant changes.

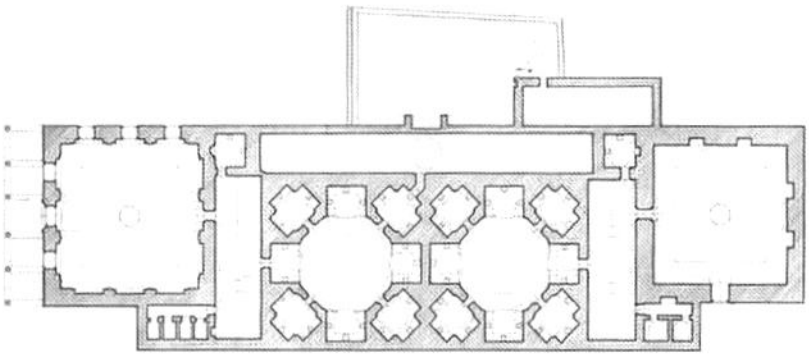

architects
Mimar Sinan / Faculty of Architecture & Design of Kocaeli University

type
hammam

construction
XVI century / 2008

03. Grand Bazaar of Istanbul

Beyazıt
34126 Fatih, Istanbul

Mon - Sun / 10 am - 6 pm
+90 212 517 35 35
dernek@kapalicarsi.org.tr
www.kapalicarsi.com.tr

36ES, 38Z > Beyazıt

T1 > Beyazıt

As in all traditional Ottoman cities, the Istanbul bazaar was not built according to plan but developed over time. With the construction of the two *bedesten* markets and the bazaars, streets and shops that grew alongside, Istanbul began to assume the characteristics of a Turkish city. The Grand Bazaar [Kapalı Çarşı] covers an area of 30,700 square metres with 61 internal streets and over 4,000 shops. The internal structure of the Bazaar is composed of arches and barrel vaulted ceilings. Each street has its individual style that varies in width and height according to the adjacent buildings. The Bazaar architecture does not reflect any specific era, but is a structure that has changed constantly according to the period and the commercial needs of the population. Therefore, the relationship between architecture, trade and territorial identity is visible, because each single element, (people or items for sale), is a fundamental component of the atmosphere of this place.

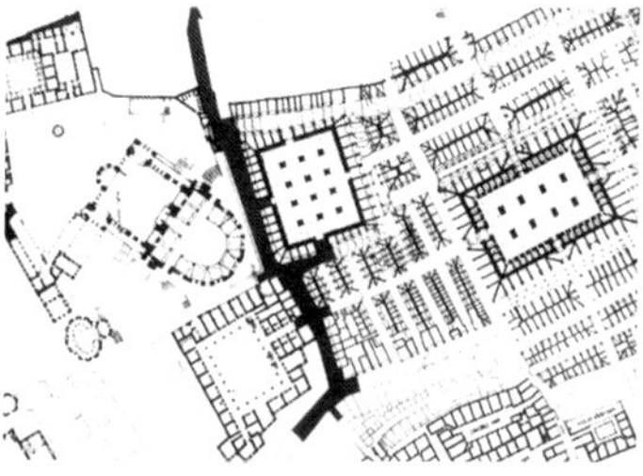

© A. Savin, Wikipedia

architects
Mehmet II

type
market

construction
1461

04. Beyazıt State Library

Beyazıt Mh.,
Çadırcılar Cd. No:4
Fatih 34126, Istanbul

open to the public
+90 212 591 12 48
kutuphane3420@ktb.gov.tr
istanbulbeyazitdevlet.
kutuphane.gov.tr

M2 > Vezneciler - İstanbul Üniversitesi

36ES, 38Z, 91E, 97 > Beyazıt Üniversite
36ES, 38Z > Beyazıt
HVIST-12 > Aksaray-Beyazıt Meydan

T1 > Beyazıt

Located in Beyazıt Square in the heart of the historic peninsula, the Beyazit Public Library [Beyazıt Devlet Kütüphanesi], founded in 1884, was the first state library in Turkey and one of the largest and oldest in Istanbul. The restoration work, which the architects defined as "minimal intervention" was aimed not simply at preserving this historic building, but also at enhancing its heritage aspects. The use of light was a fundamental element when working towards this principle. Tabanlioğlu Architects worked with Dinnebier lighting design to create a strip lighting system that runs along the base of the perimeter walls in each room, remodelling the space and giving it new depth. The lighting accentuates the surface of the stone walls while also creating a visual connection between the ancient structure and the modern elements like the new library furnishings and the glass showcases containing ancient texts. Another fundamental technique was to move the entrance into the courtyard, where the concrete roof was removed and replaced with a transparent membrane to bring light and a view of the sky within the structure.

architects
Beyazıt II / Tabanlioğlu Architects

type
library

construction
1884 / 2015

05. Istanbul University Observatory

Üniversite, Vezneciler
34452 Fatih, Istanbul

open to the public
+90 212 522 31 67
gozlemevi@istanbul.edu.tr
gozlemevi.istanbul.edu.tr/tr

M2 > Vezneciler - İstanbul Üniversitesi

36ES, 387, 91E, 97 > Beyazıt

T1 > Laleli-Üniversite

The Astronomy and Space Sciences Department was founded following the Istanbul University reform in 1933. The astronomical observatory [İstanbul Üniversitesi Gözlemevi] building was designed by the architect, Arif Hikmet Holtay and was constructed between 1934 and 1936 in the Beyazit district near the historic Beyazit Tower. The reinforced concrete building is composed of a rectangular structure that contains lecture rooms, a library, and the observation tower. In the rectangular block, a cylindrical structure supports the dome containing the famous Zeiss telescope which is still active today. This is an extremely functional building with a seemingly simple geometrical design, but with a clever balance between the vertical and horizontal structures, with their striking meticulous design. The squared-off rectangular block accentuates the cylindrical telescope tower, which is the focal point of the complex.

architects
Arif Hikmet Holtay

type
university observatory

construction
1936

06. Istanbul University Faculty of Literature

Balabanağa Mahallesi
Ordu Cad, Laleli Cd. No:6
34134 Fatih, Istanbul

open to the public
+90 212 440 00 74
edebiyatdekan@istanbul.edu.tr
edebiyat.istanbul.edu.tr/en

M2 > Vezneciler - İstanbul Ünıversıtesı

36ES, 38Z, 91E, 97 > Laleli, Beyazıt Üniversite

T1 > Laleli-Üniversite

The Istanbul University building for the Faculty of Literature [İstanbul Üniversitesi Edebiyat Fakültesi] was designed by architects Sedad Hakkı Elde and Emin Halid Onat and was built between 1942 and 1947. Eldem strongly believed in a national modern architectural style based on traditional Turkish design, but that had at the same time, an imposing and monumental aspect, as can be seen in the Arts and Sciences Faculty building. The complex is strongly focused on the essence of form and symmetry. The facades are clad in stone (in a style that recalls German Nazi architecture) interrupted at 3/4 height where the two top floors of the building are faced with a pink painted plaster finish. The entrance is composed of towering monumental stone pillars that provide a glimpse of the faculty's internal cloister. The building is topped with a traditional Turkish style roof with overhanging eaves.

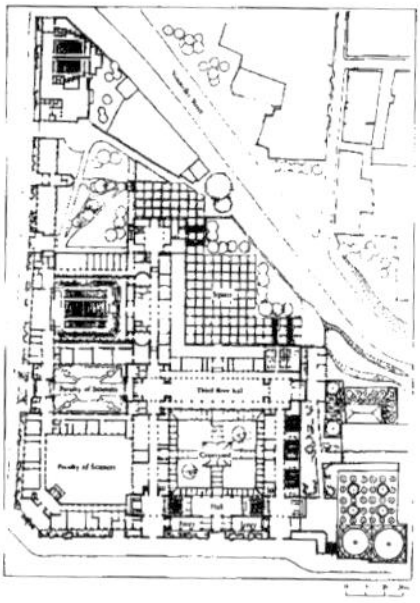

architects
Sedad Hakki Eldem,
Emin Halid Onat

type
university

construction
1947

07. Istanbul Metropolitan Municipality building

Kemal Paşa, 15 Temmuz Şehitleri Cd No:5 D:5
34134 Fatih, Istanbul

Mon - Sun / 8.30 am - 5 pm
+90 212 455 57 00
irelations@ibb.gov.tr
www.ibb.istanbul

M2 > Vezneciler - İstanbul Ünıversıtesı

Oruçgazi Ortaokulu
(bus station)

T1 > Aksaray

The building designed by Nevzat Erol'un in 1953 marks a period that was fundamental for the evolution of contemporary Turkish architecture. Together with the Hilton Hotel, built at the same time, the complex represents the first example of international style architecture in Istanbul. The municipal complex [İstanbul Büyükşehir Belediyesi Başkanlığı] is composed of two main buildings: a taller parallelepiped structure that houses administrative offices, and a lower building with ceremonial halls and meeting rooms as well as exhibition spaces, and rooms connected with the presidential office. At street level, the area between the two buildings is landscaped with large pools and fountains, as well as planted green spaces. Inside, the main council chamber has a curved ceiling in ribbed vault form to recall the dome of the Şehzade Mosque nearby. The complex is closely linked with post-war Modernist European architecture, and in a certain sense, tends more specifically towards International Style. The numerous archaeological finds that were discovered during excavation work were taken to the Archaeological Museum of Istanbul, where they are permanently on show.

architects
Nevzat Erol

type
institutional building

construction
1953

08. Museum of Istanbul

Merkezefendi
34015 Zeytinburnu, Istanbul

open to the public

A01, A10, A48, A26, A28, A30, Topkapı-Zeytinburnu, Topkapı-Kayaşehir > Topkapı

T1, T5 > Topkapı

Istanbul City Museum [İstanbul Kent Müzesi] was designed by the architectural firm, Salon Alper Derinboğaz, and is located near the Topkapi or Cannon Gate, which is part of the 5th century Theodosian walls. The museum is incorporated into the surrounding architectural context as an element that combines the concept of the ancient historic walls with the modern design of the new traffic connection system in the city. The square building resembles a single monolithic mass suspended above ground level, supported on steel pillars and glass walls. The ground floor contains public facilities including a library, conference hall, restaurants, and spaces for temporary exhibitions. The first floor of the museum houses the permanent exhibition spaces, while the workshops, service areas, storage and parking are all located in the three underground floors. The structure surrounds a central courtyard that forms the Museum Plaza, a spatial element that defines the complex since it forms the four walls around the courtyard.

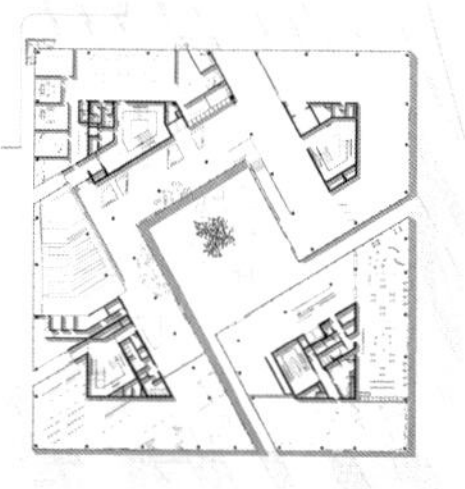

architects
Salon Alper Derinboğaz

type
museum

construction
2020

09. Aqueduct of Valens

Kalenderhane, Avrupa Yakası
34083 Fatih, Istanbul

open to the public
+90 212 455 1300

M2 > Vezneciler - İstanbul Üniversitesi

Vefa (bus station)

T1 > Aksaray

The Aqueduct of Valens [Valens Su Kemeri] was planned by the emperor Constantine after he rebuilt and expanded the city, naming it the new capital, Constantinople. It was later completed by the Emperor Valens. It is one of the few remaining ancient infrastructures to be admired in this part of the region, and played a fundamental role under Constantine's rule and successive periods, because the city suffered from a lack of water. It was essential to provide water for the increasing population and the magnificent buildings and wonderful gardens. The water was collected and then stored in vast underground cisterns like the Basilica Cistern [Yerebatan Sarnıcı], located near the Santa Sofia Basilica, and built in 532 by Justinian I on top of a pre-existant structure. Thanks to constant restoration work that has reinstated the Cistern's former beauty, today it is possible to visit and admire the enormous underground chambers, built under an ancient basilica. Today, the Basilica Cistern and the Valens Aqueduct represent unique constructions that add to the architectural stratification of Istanbul, now a totally contemporary city, but which has maintained strong ties with the history of its origins and traditions.

architects
–

type
infrastructure

construction
368

10. İMÇ – İstanbul Manifaturacılar Çarşısı

Mollahüsrev,
Mehmethan Sok. No:1
34134 Fatih, Istanbul

Mon - Sat / 7 am - 7 pm

info@imc.org.tr
www.imc.org.tr/iletisim.php

M2 > Vezneciler - İstanbul Üniversitesi

Vefa (bus station)

T1 > Sirkeci

The İMÇ complex [İstanbul Manifaturacılar Çarşısı] was designed by Dogan Tekeli and Sami Sisa in the late 1950s, a period that was characterised by the initial wave of modernisation in Istanbul. The building was the keystone for the introduction of Modernism and urban planning in the Turkish city. The evolution of this complex is especially interesting because it underwent various modifications according to the different historical changes in the city. It was originally composed of 6 blocks and housed textile shops; gradually these shops changed function and purpose, undergoing a post-planning process that followed the market trends and evolving development of Istanbul. Internal courtyards, walkways and helical stairs are all elements that contributed to the character and impact of this structure because of the careful and intelligent architectural composition. The importance of this building was confirmed by the fact it was chosen as one of the sites to host the tenth International Istanbul Biennial.

architects
Dogan Tekeli, Sami Sisa,
Metin Hepgüler

type
commercial complex

construction
1956

11. Sirkeci Health Center Social Security Supplementary Service Building

Zeyrek, İtfaiye Cd. No:54
34083 Fatih, Istanbul

Mon - Fri / 8.30 am - 5 pm
+90 212 526 52 83
unkapanisgm@sgk.gov.tr

M2 > Vezneciler - İstanbul Üniversitesi

Vefa (bus station)

T1, Kılıç Ali Paşa Hamamı > Aksaray

One of the best-known projects designed by the architect Sedad Hakki Eldem, is the Social Security Headquarters [Sirkeci Sağlık Sosyal Güvenlik Merkezi] in the Zeyrek district, built between 1962 and 1964. Constructed on a triangular site at the foot of a hill using traditional wood panels, the building has a modern aspect because of the use of standard reinforced concrete elements such as columns, struts, and foundations. The construction also includes wooden structures and projecting elements taken from local architecture, and stone features inspired by Ottoman monuments. The architect approached the question of introducing the building into the historic surroundings through a carefully integrated assimilation of the past that can be seen in the rhythm and language of the different elements and the general aspect of the building. With this project, Eldem managed to combine modernity and tradition in the same architectural design.

architects
Sedad Hakkı Eldem

type
medical and
assistance centre

construction
1964

12. PTT – Grand Post Office

Hobyar, Büyük Postane Cd. No:25
34112 Fatih, Istanbul

open to the public
+90 212 526 12 00

B1 > Marmaray Sirkeci

121CS, TB2 > Eminönü
BN1 > Eminönü İskele

T1 > Sırkecı

Eminönü-İhlas-Mudanya > Eminönü
Sirkeci-Harem > Sirkeci

The Grand Post Office [Büyük Postane] is located in the Fatih district in the Sirkeci quarter. Built between 1905 and 1909, it was designed by the architect, Mehmet Vedat Teko, and was one of the first examples of the First Turkish National Architecture style. The building has a rectangular layout, has four storeys plus a basement, and covers a surface area of 32,000 square metres. The facade sections were decorated with cut stone from Hereke, while the flooring and staircases are in marble. Local ceramic tiles were used for window sill decoration. On each side of the main facade is a clock tower, crowned with a dome and topped with a gilded roof lantern. The monumental aspect of the building is accentuated by the Ottoman decorative elements, quality materials, and entrance stairway which underline the important role played by the Grand Post Office.

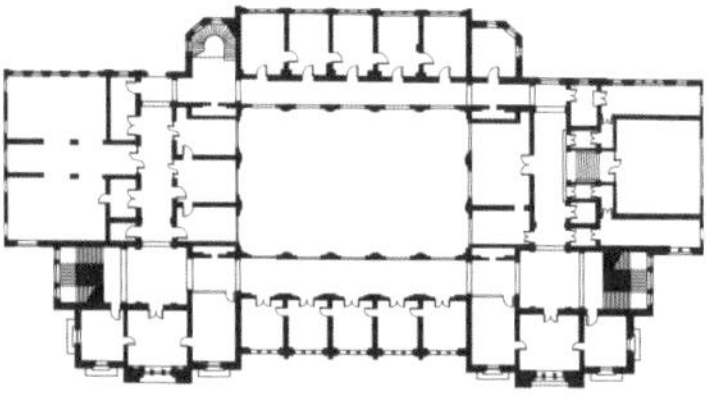

architects
Mehmet Vedat Tek

type
post office building

construction
1909

13. Topkapı Imperial Kitchens

Cankurtaran
34122 Fatih, Istanbul

Wed - Mon / 9 am - 6 pm
+90 212 512 04 80
info@millisaraylar.gov.tr
www.millisaraylar.gov.tr/saraylar/topkapi-sarayi

B1 > Marmaray Sirkeci

BN1 > Sarayburnu
TB > Sultanahmet Square

T1 > Gülhane

Eminönü-İhlas-Mudanya > Eminönü
Sirkeci-Harem > Sirkeci

The Imperial Kitchens located in the historic Topkapi Palace [Topkapı Sarayı], were first built in the 15th century and expanded in 1566 by Suleiman the Magnificent, then rebuilt by the architect, Mimar Sinan, after the fire of 1574. In 2010, the architectural firm, Teğet was chosen to design a new museum layout in this space to exhibit Ottoman culinary culture. When designing the exhibition layout, the architects paid particular attention to the beautiful Ottoman architectural structure in the Imperial Kitchens, incorporating it as an integrated part of the exhibition. This resulted in a project that was developed mainly on a horizontal plane based on a modular grid system. The first element is the raised black walkway, detached from the walls, that runs through the whole length of the kitchens, interrupted at certain points to reveal the original flooring below. The large transparent showcases are set on bases of the same surface material to create visual continuity.

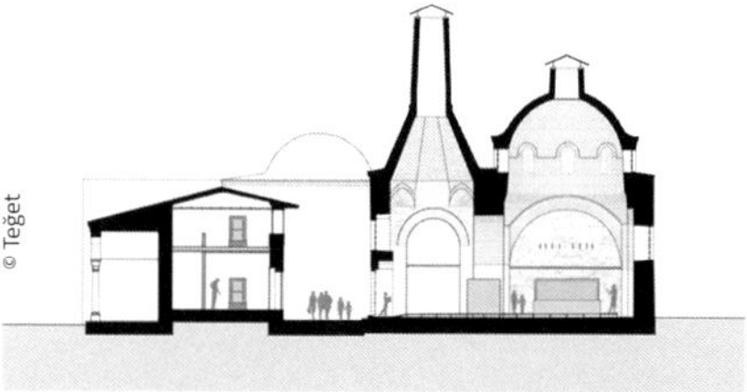

© Teğet

architects
Mimar Sinan / Teğet

type
museum

construction
1574 / 2011

14. Baghdad Kiosk

Cankurtaran
34122 Fatih, Istanbul

Wed - Mon / 9 am - 6 pm
+90 212 522 09 89
info@millisaraylar.gov.tr

B1 > Marmaray Sirkeci

BN1 > Sarayburnu

T1 > Gülhane

Eminönü-İhlas-Mudanya > Eminönü
Sirkeci-Harem > Sirkeci

The architectural style of the kiosk is based on concepts that are fundamental in understanding the traditions of Ottoman architecture. These leisure pavilions, places of pleasure and relaxation, were units that were aggregated together to form the complex of the Topkapı Palace [Topkapı Sarayı]. The Baghdad Kiosk [Bağdat Köşkü], built in 1639 to commemorate the Baghdad Campaign of Sultan Murad IV is located in the innermost courtyard of the Topkapı Palace and was reserved for the private use of the Sultan who would take his coffee there after his morning prayers. Under the rule of Selim III (1789-1807) the Kiosk was converted into a private library. The pavilion is octagonal in shape, roofed with a dome. The tiles used for the decorative narrative are one of the most refined examples of classic Ottoman production. The columns and arches of the portico are constructed in white and red marble while the ceiling is clad in wooden slats painted green. The doors, window frames and cupboard structures are made from inlaid ebony wood. The entire pavilion underwent extensive restoration in 2006 under the direction of the provincial authorities for the supervision of monuments in Istanbul. Although the side facades are blind walls, variations were introduced to the brick pattern of the internal walls between the string course bands, indicated by steel beams. The regular brick layout was interrupted by projecting elements that create different shadow effects during the day.

architects	type	construction
-	pavilion	1639

15. Legacy Ottoman Hotel

Hobyar, Hamidiye Cd. No:16
34112 Fatih, Istanbul

partially open to the public
+90 212 527 67 67
info@legacyottomanhotel.com
www.legacyottomanhotel.com

B1 > Marmaray Sirkeci

81, BN1 >
Eminönü İskele
121CS, TB2 > Eminönü

T1 > Sirkeci

Sirkeci-Harem > Sirkeci
Eminönü-İhlas-Mudanya > Eminönü

The Istanbul 4th Vakıf Han [Dördüncü Vakıf Han] was designed by the architect Kemalettin Bey, director of the Construction and Restoration Department at the Ottoman Ministry of Foundations. The construction began in 1911, but was not completed until 1926 because of the First World War. It was one of the last buildings constructed under the Ottoman Empire, and was built to satisfy the demand for office blocks. Later, during the occupation of Istanbul, the uncompleted building was used by the French troops as a barracks, under the name of Caserne Victor. Today, it houses the luxury Legacy Ottoman Hotel. The seven storey building is built in the First Turkish National Architecture style: the facades are clad in stone and decorated with silver and gold detailing. The elegant window openings define the rhythm of the facade with a different shape for each level for greater impact. One of the outstanding features of this magnificent building are the domes that crown the two turrets on each side of the facade. They are based on the design of the dome of the al-Aqsa Mosque in Jerusalem that Kemalettin Bey visited in 1919.

architects
Kemalettin Bey

type
hotel

construction
1926

16. Galata Bridge

Galata Köprüsü
34425 Beyoğlu, Istanbul

open to the public

32, 97GE, 121CS, TB > Eminönü

T1 > Eminönü, Karaköy

Kadıköy-Karaköy-Eminönü, Üsküdar-Karaköy-Eminönü > Eminönü

The Galata Bridge [Galata Köprüsü] was one of the first connections to be built between the Golden Horn and the modern part of the city of Istanbul. Architects like Leonardo da Vinci and Michelangelo Buonarroti were approached to propose a design for the project, although their ideas were never realised. The first bridge was built in 1845, followed by five further versions that reflected historical evolution and the new evolving needs of the population. The current bridge was built in 1994. It is constructed on two levels: the first upper level is designed for vehicle and pedestrian traffic, while the second level below, is designed exclusively for pedestrians and houses cafés and restaurants. The interesting aspect of this project is the method used to take advantage of a space that is normally not utilised, often an empty abandoned urban space. This concept has provided new life and a specific functional role.

architects
Fritz Leonhardt

type
infrastructure

construction
1994

Yakupağa Sk.
Işık Sk.
İstanbul Büyükşehir Belediyesi Karikatür ve Mizah Merkezi
Yapı Kredi Yayınları
Bülent Demir Cd.
Neva Sk.
Çivici Sk.
28
27
Türabi Baba Sebili
Bahriye Cd.
Refik Saydam Cd.
29
Eski Çiçekçi Sk.
Tepebaşı Cd.
Pera Müzesi
Tabanlıoğlu Architects
Camadan Sk.
Fransız Sarayı
Arıkay Sk.
Pera Palace Hotel
Suyabatmaz Demirel Architects
Turabi Baba Cd.
Akarca Sk.
32
30
Fransız Ma
Refik Saydam Cd.
Ayni Ali Baba Sk.
İstanbul Modern Sanat Müzesi
31
Hıdivyal Palas
Aybastı Sk.
Evliya Çelebi Cd.
36
Şişhane
Kumbaracı Ykş.
Örtme
Teğet
33
Beyoğlu
The Tunnel Marker
Galata Mevlevihanesu Müzesi
35
34
Galip Dede Cd.
Serdar-ı Ekrem Cd.
J
İlk Belediye Cd.
Dibek Sk.
Tutsak Sk.
Habib Gerez Sanat Evi
MArS-Architects
21
Harup Sk.
Okçu Musa Cd.
Mürver Sk.
BELTUR Galata Kulesi
20
Kemeraltı
Matbah Emini Hasan Ağa Çeşmesi
Eski Galata Surları – Azapkapı
Buğulu Sk.
19
Abdussalah Sk.
Sağlık Bilimleri Üniversitesi Rektörlüğü
Haliç Köprüsü
Necatibey Cd.
Üsküfçüler Sk.
Tersane Cd.
Arap Camii
18
Bankerhan Hotel
17
Kamondo Merdivenleri
Tarihi
Ceneviz Mahkeme Binası
Bakır Sk.
37
Alefte Hatun Çeşmesi
Karaköy Palas
Tersane Cd.
Kemankeş Cd.
Haliç
Verdizar Kadın Çeşmesi
Karaköy
Yeraltı Camii
Tarihi karakoy balikcisi
Rıhtım Cd.
0 m
100 m
250 m

Beyoğlu

17. SALT Galata
18. Camondo Stairs
19. Suma Han
20. 2F Evi
21. Ipera 25
22. Kılıç Ali Paşa Hamamı
23. Istanbul Modern
24. Studio-X
25. NoXX Apartment
26. The Museum of Innocence
27. Garaj İstanbul
28. Walk-in Cinema
29. Pera Museum
30. Borusan Art
31. Botter House
32. Soho House Istanbul
33. Beyoğlu Municipality Palace
34. Zemin Istanbul
35. Şişhane Park
36. Deniz Palas / IKSV – İstanbul Kültür Sanat Vakfi / IKSV – Alt Kat
37. Golden Horn Metro Bridge

17. SALT Galata

Azapkapı, Bankalar Cd. No:11
34421 Beyoğlu, Istanbul

Tue - Sat / 10 am - 8 pm
Sun / 12 am - 6 pm
+90 212 334 22 00
press@saltonline.org
saltonline.org

M2 > Şişhane

Perșembe Pazarı
(bus station)
26, 26A, 28, 28T, 30D, 70KE > Kemeraltı

T1 > Karaköy

F2 > Karaköy

The SALT Galata is one of the most important contemporary art galleries in the city of Istanbul. The building that houses the museum was designed for the Imperial Ottoman Bank by the French Ottoman architect, Alexandre Vallaury, in 1892. In 2011 the building was restored by the Turkish architectural firm, Mimarlar ve Han Tümertekin. The restoration project preserved the original facade, and re-designed the interior, with particular focus on the new traffic flow of visitors coming to view the exhibits. Innovative systems were used to manipulate natural daylight. The glass roofing was replaced with new rotating glass panels to regulate internal light. Glass was also used in the entrance, where the large glass wall provides a view through the whole depth of the building. As well as the exhibition space, the museum also houses a specialized library (Salt Research) designed by ȘANALarc, an auditorium, a foyer and archive space.

© ȘANALarc

architects
Alexandre Vallaury /
Mimarlar ve Han Tümertekin

type
museum

construction
1892 / 2011

18. Camondo Stairs

Bereketzade,
Bankalar Cd. No:10
34421 Beyoğlu, Istanbul

open to the public

M2 > Şişhane

Karaköy (bus station)
26, 26A, 28, 28T, 30D, 70KE > Kemeraltı

T1 > Karaköy İstasyonu

F2 > Karaköy

Eminönü-Kadıköy-Adalar, Kadıköy-Karaköy, Kadıköy-Karaköy-Eminönü, Üsküdar-Karaköy-Eminönü > Karaköy

The Camondo Stairs [Kamondo Merdivenleri] were built between 1870 and 1880 by Abraham Salomon Camondo. Two curving white masonry staircases intersect and separate like fabric draped between two tall buildings. The geometry is an eclectic combination of Neoclassical and Empire styles and is an example of unusual beauty that attracts the attention of passers-by. An empty urban space was used to create an elegant and unique structure that transmits the beauty of a period and recalls a famous banking dynasty, the Camondo family, one of the most important in Istanbul. They were responsible for setting up a new banking system and were also strong promoters of modernising the urban, architectural and cultural infrastructures of the city.

architects
Abraham Salomon Camondo

type
monument

construction
1880

19. Suma Han

Yanıkkapı Sk. No:3
34421 Beyoğlu, Istanbul

open to the public
+90 212 706 78 62
contact@suma.com.tr
www.suma.com.tr

M2 > Şişhane, Haliç

Perşembe Pazarı
(bus station)

F2 > Karaköy

Eminönü-Kadıköy-Adalar, Eminönü Kadıköy-Karaköy, Kadıköy-Karaköy-Eminönü, Üsküdar-Karaköy-Eminönü > Karaköy

© MArS-Architects

The building that now houses the Suma Han space was built in 1902 in a former Genoese district as a *reki* distillery, later converted to a printing firm. In the 1940s, the building was bought by Andon Kasapoglu, who left it to his family. In the late 1990s, the following generation changed its function, and in 2009, it was opened as a multi-functional space. The management of Suma Han was assumed by the art critic and curator, Beral Madra, of the BM Suma Contemporary Arts Center. The Suma Han is a fascinating space, brimming with overlaid architectural styles that do not dominate one another, but communicate to form a unique and creative atmosphere. It is a vast, constantly changing space that uses its traditional Turkish structure to create something new and unusual. Its flexibility allows the space to be continuously transformed according to the demands of the moment. The multi-function building can morph into art studios, musical events, fashion shows, and even contains rental apartments.

architects
MArS-Architects

type
exhibition space

construction
2009

20. 2F Evi

Şahkulu, Şahkapısı Sk. No:6
34421 Beyoğlu, Istanbul

partially open to the public

M2 > Şişhane

26, 26A, 26B, 28, 28T, 30D, 70D, 70KE > Kemeraltı

F2 > Beyoğlu

2F Evi is a 19th century building located opposite the Galata Tower. The intervention by the Turkish architectural firm, Mimarlar ve Han Tümertekin, was focused on changing the building's function. The building houses a vast collection of contemporary art, and a library, as well as temporary accommodation. The huge glass windows installed on the main facade provide a constant dialogue with the Galata Tower and spectacular views of the panorama. The transversal cross section is composed of a play of solids and voids: the atrium and the library have double height ceilings, and the library faces a vertical green wall at the back of the building. To create this striking element, the architects created a kind of green path, an open element that slices the structure vertically for a height of five floors. This design feature was able to increase daylight and natural ventilation within the building.

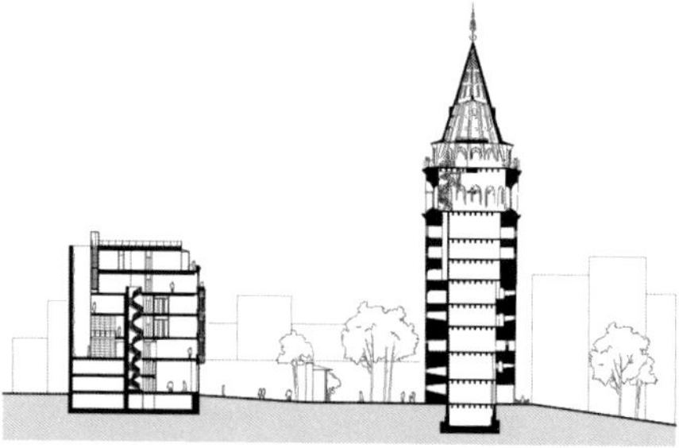

architects
Mimarlar ve Han Tümertekin

type
cultural centre

construction
2010

21. Ipera 25

Müeyyedzade,
Tatar Beyi Sk. No:25
34425 Beyoğlu, Istanbul

external viewing only

M2 > Şişhane

26, 26A, 26B, 28, 28T, 30D, 70D, 70KE > Kemeraltı

T2 > Beyoğlu Tünel

F2 > Beyoğlu

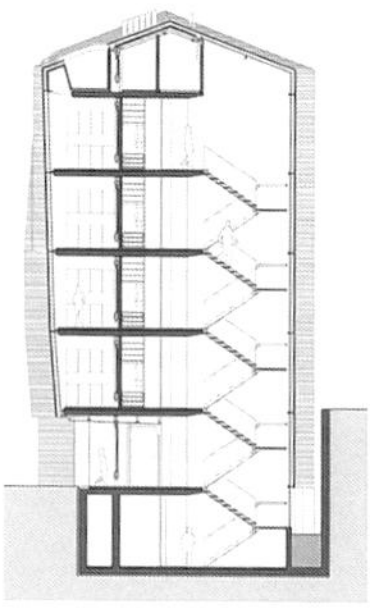

© Ahmet Alataş Workshop

The residential building, Ipera 25, designed by the architectural firm, Ahmet Altas Workshop, is slotted between other old buildings in the Galata district, interrupting all visual, stylistic, or construction material continuity with the pre-existing buildings. Its strongly contemporary aspect is expressed on the two facades composed of steel and glass structures, shielded by a screen of wooden louvered shutters that create an unusual link between the domestic environment and the street. These two facades are enclosed between two reinforced concrete blind walls. The architectural design is even more interesting on the main facade where the structure is divided into four vertical sections to generate movement; certain segments project outwards in different points to form triangular shapes creating lateral openings to bring natural daylight into the interiors.

architects
Ahmet Alataş Workshop

type
residential building

construction
2011

22. Kılıç Ali Paşa Hamamı

Kemankeş Karamustafa Paşa, Hamam Sk. No:1
34425 Beyoğlu, Istanbul

Mon - Sun / 8 am - 4 pm,
4.30 pm - 11.30 pm
+90 212 393 80 10
info@kilicalipasahamami.com
kilicalipasahamami.com

M2 > Şişhane

Tophane (bus station)
121CS > Galataport

T1 > Tophane
T2 > Beyoğlu Tünel

F2 > Karaköy

Haliç-Hattı, Kadıköy-Karaköy-Eminönü, Üsküdar-Karaköy-Eminönü > Karaköy

This historic Hamam was one of a group of buildings constructed as part of a larger *külliye* complex in the Tophane quarter in the Beyoğlu district. The original project was designed by the renowned architect, Sinan, and was built around 1580. Over the centuries, additions and reconstructions for functional reasons led to deterioration and the building lost its identity and original layout, until it remained derelict and abandoned. In 2011, the Cafer Bozkurt Architecture team was commissioned to re-establish the original function of the hamam, and was asked to restore the former authentic 16th century layout. All the pre-existing construction carried out in the 1950s was removed from the two dome-roofed central rooms whose spatial layout had been compromised. This work led to the rediscovery of the traditional stone divans set against the walls. A wooden structure was built in the main rooms to create a raised gallery to house changing rooms and bathroom services for clients, without disrupting the overall appearance of the general space. The technical services were housed in a new galvanised steel construction set in the garden to the rear of the building in order to preserve the integrity of the hamam structure, even from the exterior.

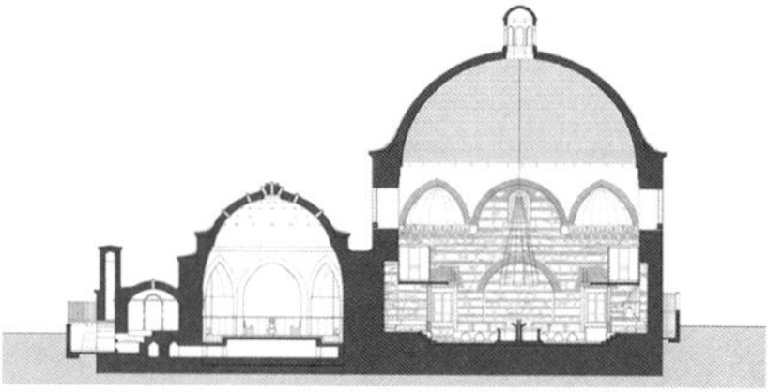

architects
Mimar Sinan /
Cafer Bozkurt Architecture

type
hamam

construction
1581 / 2011

23. Istanbul Modern

Kılıçali Paşa,
Tophane İskele Cd. No:1/1
34433 Beyoğlu, Istanbul

open to the public
+90 212 334 7300
info@istanbulmodern.org
www.istanbulmodern.org

Tophane (bus station)
121CS > Galataport

T1 > Tophane

Haliç-Hattı, Kadıköy-Karaköy-Eminönü, Üsküdar-Karaköy-Eminönü > Karaköy

The project for the new Istanbul Modern Museum began in 2016. Renzo Piano Building Workshop collaborated with Arup Istanbul on a project to replace the existing structure with a new museum able to redefine the urban space between the old city to the west, the Bosphorus in the south, the Tophane park to the north and the new Galata seafront development to the east. The museum project reflects the overall master plan built along the 1.5 kilometre length of the Bosphorus shore, redefining the Galata connection with the seafront. The museum complex has five floors, two of which are below ground, while on street level, an enclosed area provides access to a café-bar and the route through the sculpture garden. With a surface of 15,000 square metres, the new Istanbul Modern can cater not only to permanent and temporary exhibitions, but is also open to the public for recreational and cultural activities, as well as educational and experimental workshops in the "Discovery Space". The concrete structure facades are clad with metal panels that vibrate to reflect light. An additional structure on the main building facade contains the emergency stairways in continuous external routes positioned to bridge the exhibition spaces and the areas overlooking the Bosphorus.

architects
Renzo Piano
Building Workshop

type
museum

construction
2004

24. Studio-X

Pürtelaş Hasan Efendi Mahallesi, Meclis-i Mebusan Cd. No:35
34427 Beyoğlu, Istanbul

Tue - Fri / 10.30 am - 1 pm,
2 pm - 6 pm
Sat / 2 pm - 6 pm
+90 212 292 07 47
studioxistanbul@columbia.edu
www.studio-xistanbul.org/en/space

26, 26A, 26B, 28, 28T, 30D, 70D, 70KE > Salıpazarı

T1 > Fındıklı Mimar Sinan Üniversitesi

Studio-X is an urban laboratory created by Mark Wigley aimed at carrying out global urban and architectural research on the future of cities. It provides creative spaces for generating original ideas on the subject of urban development. The first Studio-X was set up in New York and further centres were opened in Rio de Janeiro, Mumbai, Beijing, Johannesburg and Istanbul. The Istanbul studio was opened in 2013, and is located on the ground floor of a building in Beyoğlu. Designed to create an open, light-filled space, a full length glass wall was installed between the Studio-X workspace and the street front. The internal space is spread over two floors. Openings were cut into the upstairs flooring to create a double height space for greater interaction with the ground floor. The building hosts exhibitions, workshops and conferences that can be held simultaneously or separately. For this reason, the internal space has been organised to be used in a flexible, unrestricted manner, assuming different configurations and layouts according to necessity.

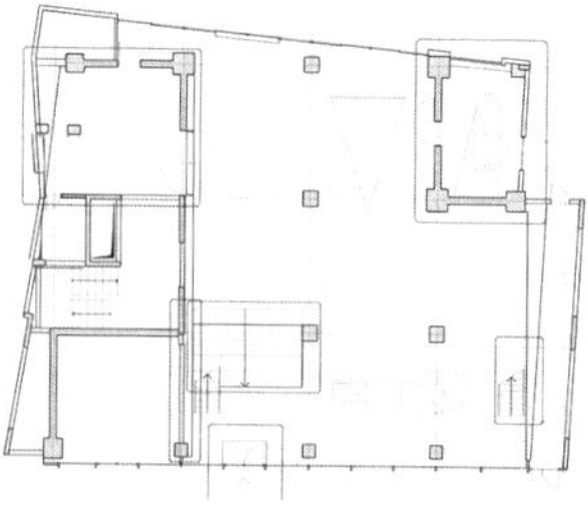

© Superpool

© Serkan Taycan

architects	type	construction
Superpool	offfices, cultural centre	2013

25. NoXX Apartment

Güllabici Sk. No:20
34433 Beyoğlu, Istanbul

external viewing only

M2 > Taksim

26, 26A, 26B, 28, 28T, 30D, 70D, 70KE >
Salıpazarı
Tophane (bus station)

T2 > Hüseyin Ağa Camii

F1 > Taksım

The Cihangir quarter in the Beyoğlu district, located between Taksim Square and Kabataş, is a vibrant neighbourhood of small apartment buildings, stores and cafés. The CM Mimarlık architecture team was asked to design a multi storey apartment building for several families in a narrow dead end street, in a short space of time. The steel frame structure was inserted between two pre-existing buildings and was left exposed, to maintain its industrial character. The voids in the steel frame facades were filled with exposed brick walls. Underground, the foundations were cast in reinforced concrete. The complex is divided into seven apartments that vary in size between 60 and 70 square metres, including two duplex apartments, and another two-floor attic apartment with an adjoining garden. The facade overlooking the street is a full glass curtain wall punctuated by a regular grid of window frames made from the same coloured steel as the building's steel support structure.

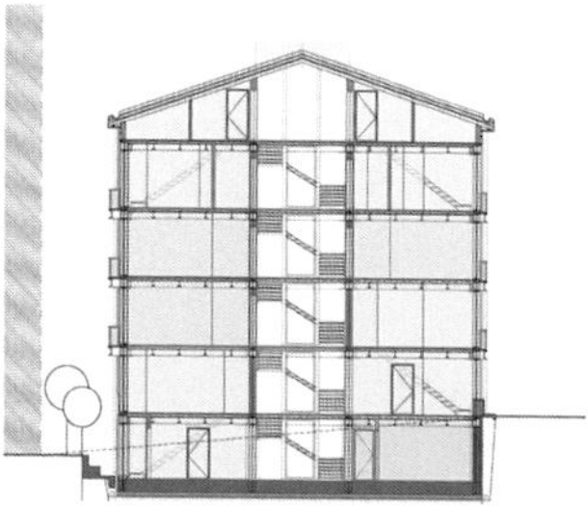

© CM Mimarlık

architects
CM Mimarlık

type
residential complex

construction
2013

26. The Museum of Innocence

Çukurcuma Cad.,
Firuzağa, Dalgıç Çk. No:2
34425 Beyoğlu, Istanbul

Tue - Wed, Fri - Sun /
10 am - 6 pm
Thu / 10 am - 9 pm
+90 212 252 97 38
info@masumiyetmuzesi.org
tr.masumiyetmuzesi.org

M2 > Şişhane

Tophane (bus station)

T2 > Odakule, Akflr
T1 > Tophane

F2 > Beyoğlu

An old, red-painted house stands on a corner in the Beyoğlu district, in a neighbourhood famous for its antique shops, attracting the attention of passers-by; it is the Museum of Innocence [Masumiyet Müzesi], designed by MArS-Architects. It was opened in 2012 as a literary museum, and was conceived by literary Nobel prize winner, Orhan Pamuk, alongside his book of the same title, first published in 2008. The famous Turkish writer began collecting objects in 1990 with the aim of setting up a museum that would faithfully reflect the contents of his book. The novel and the museum offer an insight into middle class life in Istanbul between 1970 and 2000. The different objects arranged inside the building follow a narrative order: each section corresponds to a chapter of the book. The author's objective is unusual and innovative; he has created a realistic world that pays homage to the concept of a museum, collecting objects charged with historical and emotional affinity. At the same time, he creates a way to play with the imagination and sensitivity of the reader and the visitor. Pamuk's project also proposes food for thought for designers who are forced to face a challenge, transforming literature into architecture.

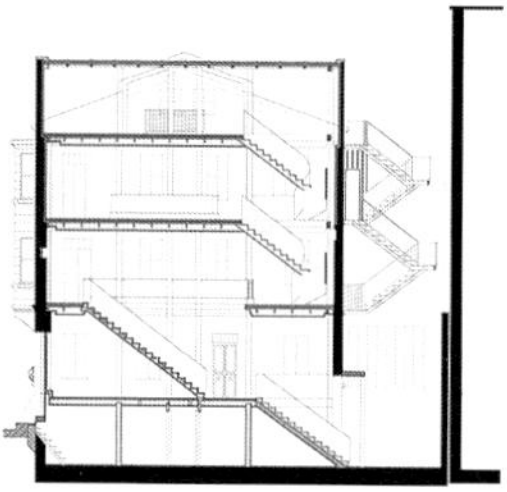

© MArS-Architects

architects
MArS-Architects

type
museum

construction
2012

27. Garaj İstanbul

Tomtom, Kaymakam Reșat Bey Sok. 11A
34433 Beyoğlu, Istanbul

open to the public
+90 212 2444499
info@garajistanbul.org
www.garajistanbul.org

M2 > Şișhane

T2 > Odakule, Galatasaray Lisesi, Akf

F2 > Beyoğlu

An old garage building in the Beyoğlu district has been converted into a new multi-functional space dedicated to art, music and dance. The Garaj İstanbul project, designed by the MArS-Architects architectural firm, was built in 2005. The interior design is closely linked with the image of the cultural space and the public who uses it. The structure is divided into two large spaces: the first houses a kind of underground foyer and a bar area, while the second is a large open space with a performing stage. The need for open spaces that can hold as many spectators as possible inspired the architects to use materials, and above all colours, as the main defining elements. A back-lit pink fluo wall, and electric blue under-floor lighting for the dance floor give the space a unique style, very different from other similar places in the city. Garaj İstanbul has become a point of reference in Istanbul for artistic circles and art and music lovers.

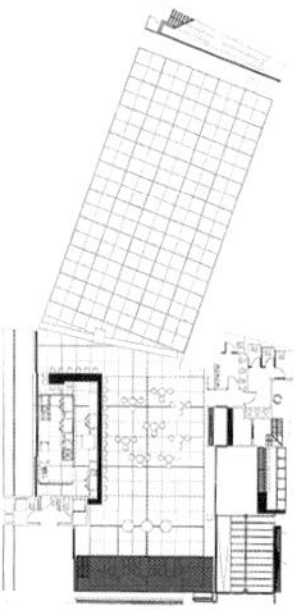

© MArS-Architects

architects
MArS-Architects

type
cultural centre

construction
2005

28. Walk-in Cinema

Asmalı Mescit,
İstiklal Cd. No:136
34430 Beyoğlu, Istanbul

open to the public
+90 212 334 22 00
press@saltonline.org

M2 > Şişhane

T2 > Odakule, Galatasaray Lisesi, Akf

F2 > Beyoğlu

The Walk-in Cinema, designed in 2011 by the Turkish architectural firm, Suyabatmaz Demirel Architects, is located inside one of the most important and active cultural centres in Istanbul, the SALT Beyoğlu building. The cinema, (also used for other events) was designed as an open space, as suggested by the lack of doors, and connects directly with the street as an invitation to passers-by to enter and spend some time. It is a clever continuous play between inside and out, between closed and open space. The material used for the internal floor paving is similar to that of the adjacent street, suggesting a continuous space, giving the impression of wanting to eliminate the idea of a "threshold". The only element that indicates it is a cinema is the slightly downward sloping floor. The Walk-in Cinema is a flexible open space whose form and function can be adapted according to different necessities and occasions. In fact, the seating units are mounted on rails and can be moved horizontally to form new seating combinations, or can be pushed to the sides to create a large single internal space in the centre.

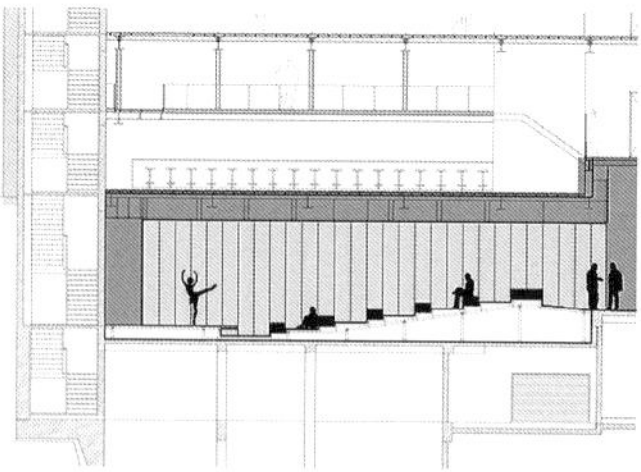

© Orhun Ülgen

architects
Suyabatmaz Demirel Architects

type
cinema

construction
2011

29. Pera Museum

Asmalı Mescit,
Meşrutiyet Cd. No:65
34430 Beyoğlu, Istanbul

Tue - Thu, Sat / 10 am - 7 pm
Fri / 10 am - 10 pm
Sun / 12 am - 6 pm
+ 90 212 334 99 00
info@peramuzesi.org.tr
www.peramuzesi.org.tr

M2 > Şişhane

T2 > Odakule, Galatasaray Lisesi, Akf

F2 > Beyoğlu

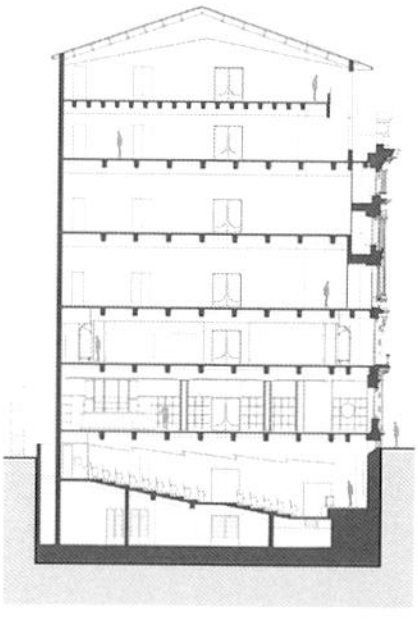

The Pera Museum [Pera Müzesi], opened in 2005, is a private museum founded by Suna and İnan Kıraç, and is located in the historic building of the former Bristol Hotel designed by the architect, Achille Manoussos, in 1893. It was renovated for the museum conversion by the architect, Sinan Gemin, who decided not to change the original facade in Neoclassical style designed by Manoussos, but to restore it and limit transformations to the interior. The main interventions made inside the building were focused on structures involving staircases and elevators, services, and the division of the various internal layouts. The modern materials used internally are in striking contrast with the traditional facade. There are five floors above ground and two below. The first floor houses the auditorium and the foyer while the upper floors house a museum. It is used as a museum and space for international exhibitions. The museum levels are divided into two galleries per floor, decorated in different colours and materials to identify the individual collections.

architects
Achille Monoussos /
Sinan Genim

type
museum

construction
1893 / 2005

30. Borusan Art

Asmalı Mescit, İstiklal Cd
Orhan Adli Apaydın Sk. No:1
34433 Beyoğlu, Istanbul

Mon - Fri / 9.30 am - 6 pm
+90 212 7058700

www.borusansanat.com

M2 > Şişhane

T2 > Odakule,
Beyoğlu Tünel

F2 > Beyoğlu

The intervention carried out by the GAD Architecture team involves the renovation of the interior of a six-floor building on İstiklal Caddesi, built in 1875. The Neoclassical facade was left intact while the project was directed at the total redesigning of the accesses and spatial layout within the historic building of Borusan Art [Borusan Sanat]. The strategy was aimed at choosing a construction system able to take maximum advantage of the internal space as a concert theatre. Flexibility in this renewed space and the integration of new functions was facilitated by the construction of a diagrid of steel beams attached to the existing wall structures around the perimeter of the building, hidden behind the Neoclassical facade. This permitted the removal of the internal partitions on each floor, leaving large areas free for use as exhibition space or for concerts. The new diagrid system can be seen from the exterior, not only thanks to clever lighting schemes that filter through the openings in the historic facade, but also at roof level, where open terraces on different levels provide widespread views of the Bosphorus.

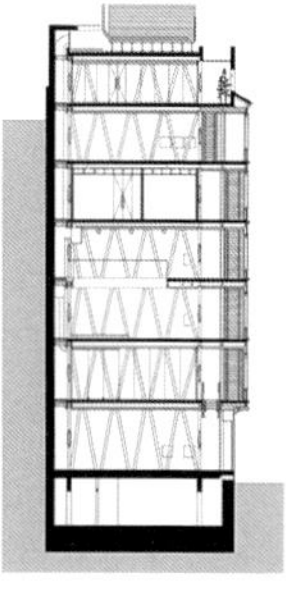

© GAD Architecture

architects
GAD Architecture

type
cultural centre

construction
2009

31. Botter House

Şahkulu, İstiklal Cd. No:235
34421 Beyoğlu, Istanbul

external viewing only

M2 > Şişhane

Şişhane 1 / Şişhane 2
(bus station)

T2 > Beyoğlu Tünel

F2 > Beyoğlu

At the beginning of the 20th century, Raimondo D'Aronco (1857-1932) was commissioned by the Dutch tailor, Jan Botter, to design a private residence and business premises on İstiklal Caddesi in the vibrant Beyoğlu district. In a coeval urban context rich in examples of the Western Art Nouveau style, D'Aronco designed a project aimed at combining western and local cultures. By constructing the building on an irregular narrow site, the facade on İstiklal Caddesi recalls the same experiments that D'Aronco had undertaken in other Italian and Turkish projects a few years before. The influence of Art Nouveau on the main facade is clear: the four half-pilasters, the framing of the string courses and the delicately "flowered" windows, with their ornamental moulded floral decoration composed of roses, corollas, and entwined organic elements, is repeated in the cast iron parapets with their similar curving sinuous design. Unlike the trends of the same period, where inserts in the facade were decorated with elements in various materials such as ceramic or glass mosaics, in this case, D'Aronco decided to continue in the same coherent style, to give the impression that the decorative elements had been modelled directly from the same structural elements as the building's bearing walls.

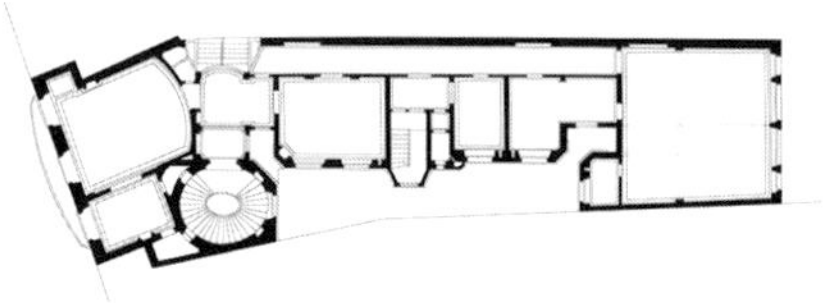

architects
Raimondo D'Aronco

type
cultural centre

construction
1900

32. Soho House Istanbul

Evliya Çelebi,
Meşrutiyet Cd. No:56
34430 Beyoğlu, Istanbul

partially open to the public
+90 212 377 71 00
info@sohohouse.com
sohohouseistanbul.com

M2 > Şişhane

Şişhane 1 / Şişhane 2
(bus station)

T2 > Beyoğlu Tünel

F2 > Beyoğlu

The famous Soho House Club is located in the historic Palazzo Corpi, commissioned by Ignazio Corpi and designed by the Italian architect, Giacomo Leoni, in 1873. The building became home to the US Embassy in 1906, and then to the US Consulate from 1937 to 2003. In 2014, Nick Jones, the founder of Soho House, decided to create a club in the Italian villa, and began restoration work. The intervention was mainly focused on restoring the original frescoes and decorations, together with careful modernising of the building. The interior decorating project was coordinated by the designer James Waterworth who worked with a group of sixteen artists. The strategy was to choose modern furnishings to create a well-balanced combination of tradition and innovation, without either aspect excessively dominating the other. The interior decor is a rich harmonious blend of pre-existing features and a range of different styles throughout, using traditional Turkish materials, rugs, and fabrics made by local artisans.

architects
Giacomo Leoni /
James Waterworth

type
hotel

construction
1873 / 2014

33. Beyoğlu Municipality Palace

Şahkulu, Constitutionalism Chad No:121
34420 Beyoğlu, Istanbul

partially open to the public

beyoglu.bel.tr/duyuru-haberler

M2 > Şişhane

Şişhane 1 / Şişhane 2
(bus station)

T2 > Beyoğlu Tünel

F2 > Beyoğlu

The Beyoğlu Municipality building [Beyoğlu Belediyesi], located in the Beyoğlu district, was commissioned by the Ottoman Sultan, Abdul-Hamid II, and built in 1885. This is not simply an impressive building, but was the first town hall in the city of Istanbul. The Beyoğlu district has a long history of cultural initiatives and innovative architecture, and has always represented the modern image of the city. The architectural intervention by Erginoğlu & Çalışlar Mimarlik comprised the conservation and restoration of the structure and the construction of new additional buildings to create a modern "municipality campus". There are three additional structures. The first is an office space building on the left; the second, on the right, is composed of a communications centre and canteen, and the third is a transparent cube that connects the Municipal Building and the second block. A further intervention by Erginoğlu & Çalışlar Mimarlik was carried out on the roof construction built in the 1980s. The whole roof was removed and replaced by a steel and glass structure that echoes the architectural style of the original period in order to maintain the compositional balance of the building's facade.

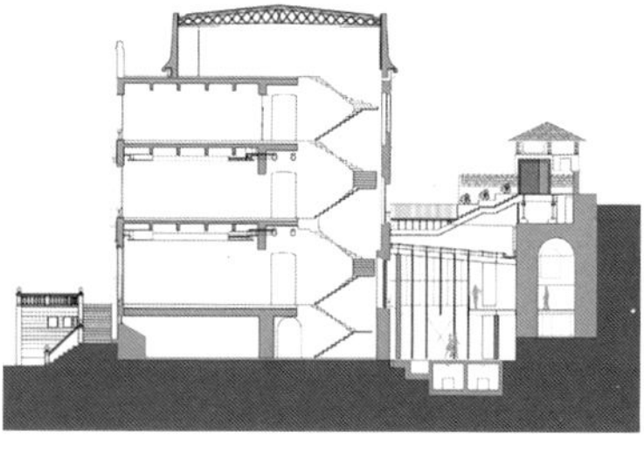

© Erginoğlu & Çalışlar Mimarlık

architects
Erginoğlu & Çalışlar Mimarlık

type
istitutional building

construction
1885 / 2013

34. Zemin Istanbul

Şahkulu, Şişhane Metro Durağı, Meşrutiyet Cd. Vergi Dairesi Girişi No:125 D:1.Kat
34421 Beyoğlu, Istanbul

Mon - Sun / 9 am - 10 pm
+90 212 449 9849
info@zeministanbul.ist
zeministanbul.ist

M2 > Şişhane

Şişhane 1 / Şişhane 2
(bus station)

T2 > Beyoğlu Tünel

F2 > Beyoğlu

The Zemin Istanbul project, designed by the Superpool architectural team in 2016, is located in a vast tunnel in the metro system near the Şişhane Metro stop, and occupies an area of about 1000 square metres. The space has been converted to house creative workshops, exhibition spaces, and meeting rooms. The largest problem faced by the architects was the permanent lack of natural light which inspired them to focus on providing a spacious airy environment. This was achieved by designing a 7 metre high space in a single, two storey open structure, interrupted by double height partitions to create internal courtyards. This play of voids and solids has prevented the feeling of a static environment, and has created a dynamic space with unexpected perspectives and views that provide a sense of distance.

© Superpool

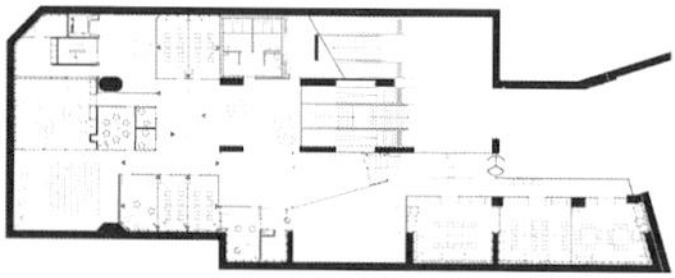

architects
Superpool

type
multi-purpose space

construction
2016

35. Şışhane Park

Emekyemez, Yolcuzade İskender Cd. No:48
34421 Beyoğlu, Istanbul

open to the public
+90 212 358 02 04

M2 > Şişhane

Şişhane 1 / Şişhane 2
(bus station)
Şişhane Minibüs
(bus station)

T2 > Şişhane

F2 > Beyoğlu

Şışhane Park, built in 2014 by the Turkish architectural firm, ŞANALarc, is situated between Beyoğlu and Tarlabaşı Road, on a site that previously housed a fire station. The aim was to provide an access route to the Galata district while creating a new focal point and public space for social and cultural activities. The project is designed with strong bold lines, and takes advantage of the different road levels to integrate viewing platforms and planted terraces. These features, and the use of different materials, add to the impact, making this park a popular centre with the local population. Thanks to its great flexibility, the park can host cultural and musical events, although this is not its only function. Şışhane Park is also a six floor underground car park, one of the first in Istanbul. The open-air space and the car park are a cleverly designed project with strong impact. Form and colour were used to identify the different car park levels, with efficient lighting to ensure that all routes inside the car park are well-lit, safe and reassuring. Şışhane Park is an innovative public space project, unique in the architectural panorama of Istanbul.

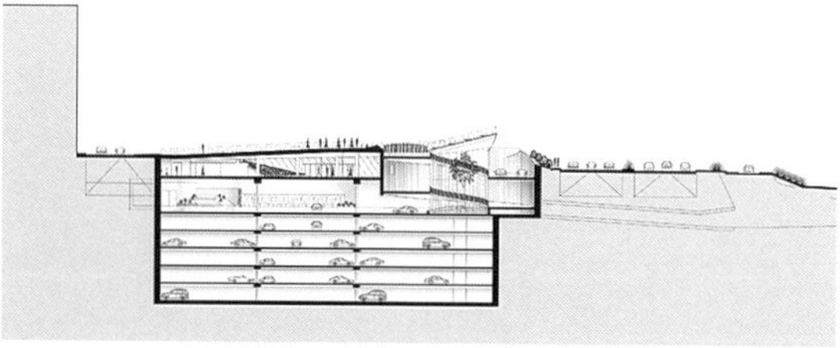

© ŞANALarc

architects
ŞANALarc

type
park, public space

construction
2014

36. Deniz Palas / IKSV – İstanbul Kültür Sanat Vakfi / IKSV – Alt Kat

Evliya Çelebi,
Sadi Konuralp Cd. No:5/2
34200 Beyoğlu, Istanbul

Mon - Fri / 9.30 am - 6 pm
+90 212 334 07 00
info@iksv.org
www.iksv.org / www.iksv.org/en/iksv-alt-kat

M2 > Şişhane

Şişhane 1 / Şişhane 2
(bus station)

T2 > Beyoğlu Tünel

F2 > Beyoğlu

The Deniz Palas, located very close to the Şişhane Metro exit, was built in 1920 by the architect, Georges Couloutros, in Art Nouveau style according to the taste of the period and has remained unchanged until today. The building was one of the first built in reinforced concrete. In 2005 the Saruhan Mimarlık architectural firm carried out conservation restoration on both the facade and the internal decorations. The building has a total floor area of 3,751 square metres. The interior is divided into office spaces, retail areas, a cafeteria, workshop, and exhibition space for artistic activities. The goal is to make the Deniz Palas a major international cultural centre for Istanbul. Since 2006 it has been home to the IKSV – İstanbul Kültür Sanat Vakfı, the Foundation created in 1973 by Nejat Eczacıbaşı. Today, the IKSV is the most important cultural, artistic and architectural institution in Istanbul, regularly organising music, art and architectural festivals, including the Turkish Pavilion at the international Venice art and architecture Bienniale.Designed by Superpool, IKSV – Alt Kat, located inside the headquarters of the Istanbul Foundation for Culture and Arts, is a large room about 150 square metres in area. It was created as part of a financial support program for children and teenagers. The area will house events such as workshops, educational programs on art, music, theatre, and films, as well as conferences and exhibitions. The room was designed to be versatile and efficient in order to cater for the activities it will host. For this reason, it was necessary to create a division between the spaces, while maintaining an airy spacious atmosphere at the same time. Collaboration with the glass manufacturers, Billur Cam Endüstrisi (BCE Glass) was fundamental in creating an installation called Flare: it is composed of an undulating laminated glass partition along the whole length of the room, attached to the ceiling with metal hooks. This sinuous transparent partition is the dominant element in the decor.

architects
Deniz Palas: Georges Couloutros / IKSV – İstanbul Kültür Sanat Vakfi: Saruhan Mimarlık / IKSV – Alt Kat: Superpool

type
museum, cultural centre

construction
Deniz Palas: 1920 / IKSV – İstanbul Kültür Sanat Vakfi: 2005 / IKSV – Alt Kat: 2019

37. Golden Horn Metro Bridge

Azapkapı
34050 Beyoğlu, Istanbul

open to the public

M2 > Haliç

47, 47E, 47K, 50E, 54E, 54TE, 77Ç > Eminönü

The Golden Horn Metro Bridge [Haliç Metro Köprüsü] is the fourth bridge on the Golden Horn. It was built between 2009 and 2014 by a consortium of the Italian construction company, Astaldi, and the Turkish architectural firm, Gülermak Ağır Sanayi İnşaat ve Taahhüt A.Ş. The viaduct was created to allow the M2 Metro line to continue its route connecting the districts of Betoğlu and Fatih. Two Metro stations are located at each end of the bridge with a third in the centre. The cable-stayed bridge covers a length of 936 metres. Although it is an infrastructure designed using contemporary criteria, the two steel supporting towers, 65 metres tall, recall the shape of a minaret: the tall slender towers that rise to the sky in almost every mosque. The minaret style towers create a visual and symbolic link with the urban context. The project includes a swing bridge that rotates on itself by 90 degrees to allow the passage of large ships.

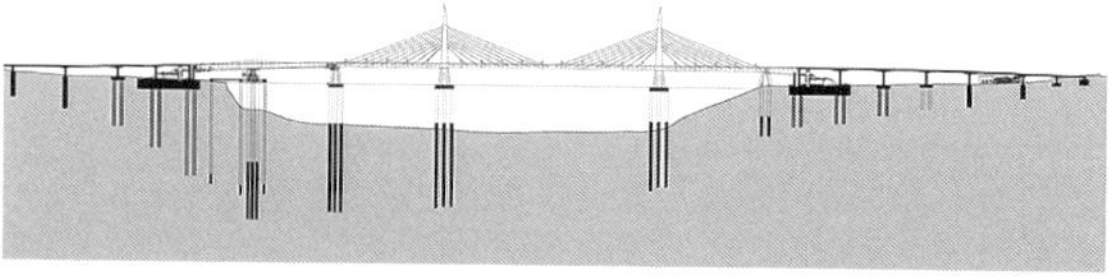

architects
Astaldi, Gülermak Ağır Sanayi
İnşaat ve Taahhüt A.Ş.

type
infrastructure

construction
2014

Beşiktaş - Şişli

38. Now Bomonti
39. Alt art space
40. Trump Cadde
41. Loft Gardens
42. Tekfen Tower
43. Levent Loft
44. Zorlu Levent
45. Kanyon
46. Demir Demirgil Theatre Hall

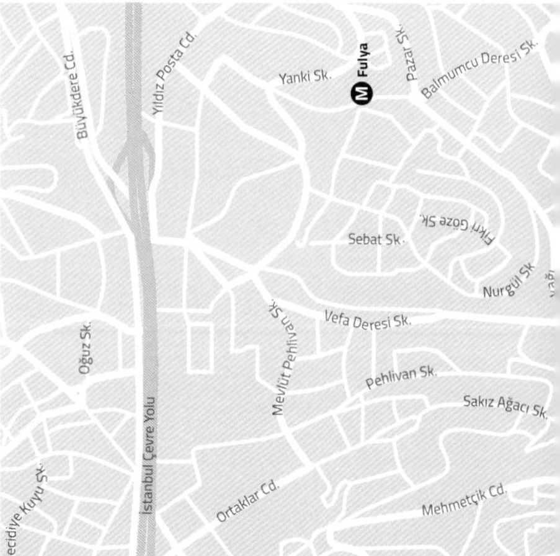

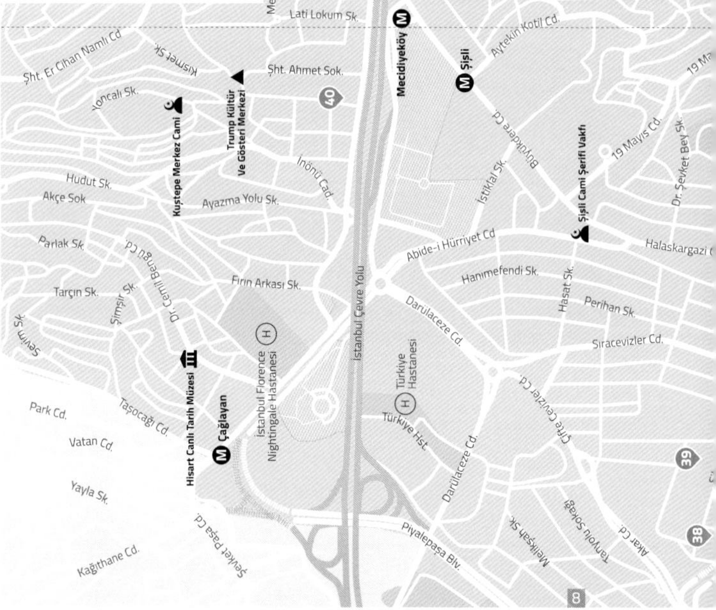

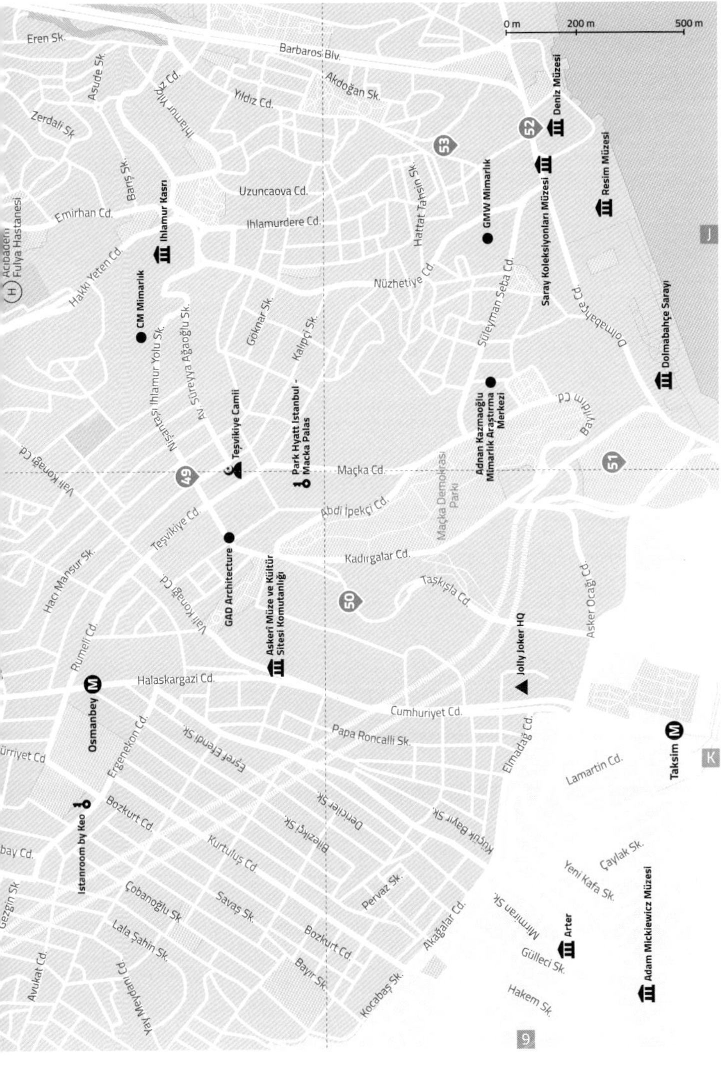
0 m
200 m
500 m
Eren Sk.
Barbaros Blv.
Asude Sk.
Ihlamur Yıldız Cd.
Yıldız Cd.
Akdoğan Sk.
Zerdali Sk.
Deniz Müzesi
52
53
Resim Müzesi
Barış Sk.
Ihlamur Kasrı
Uzuncaova Cd.
Hattat Tahsin Sk.
GMW Mimarlık
Saray Koleksiyonları Müzesi
Emirhan Cd.
Ihlamurdere Cd.
Fulya Hastanesi
Hakkı Yeten Cd.
CM Mimarlık
Nüzhetiye Cd.
Süleyman Seba Cd.
Dolmabahçe Cd.
Dolmabahçe Sarayı
J
Göknar Sk.
Kalıpçı Sk.
Nişantaşı Ihlamur Yolu Sk.
Av. Süreyya Ağaoğlu Sk.
Teşvikiye Camii
Park Hyatt Istanbul - Macka Palas
Adnan Kazmaoğlu Mimarlık Araştırma Merkezi
Bayıldım Cd.
Maçka Cd.
49
51
Vali Konağı Cd.
Abdi İpekçi Cd.
Maçka Demokrasi Parkı
Teşvikiye Cd.
GAD Architecture
Kadırgalar Cd.
Hacı Mansur Sk.
Askeri Müze ve Kültür Sitesi Komutanlığı
50
Taşkışla Cd.
Vali Konağı Cd.
Asker Ocağı Cd.
Jolly Joker HQ
Rumeli Cd.
Halaskargazi Cd.
M
Osmanbey
Cumhuriyet Cd.
Papa Roncalli Sk.
Ergenekon Cd.
Eşref Efendi Sk.
Elmadağ Cd.
M
Taksim
K
Lamartin Cd.
Istanroom by Keo
Bozkurt Cd.
Dericiler Sk.
Bilezikçi Sk.
Küçük Bayır Sk.
Kurtuluş Cd.
Çaylak Sk.
Yeni Kafa Sk.
Çobanoğlu Sk.
Savaş Sk.
Pervaz Sk.
Adam Mickiewicz Müzesi
Akağalar Cd.
Mimiran Sk.
Arter
Lala Şahin Sk.
Bozkurt Cd.
Gülleci Sk.
Bayır Sk.
Hakem Sk.
Avukat Cd.
Yay Meydanı Cd.
Kocabaş Sk.
G

Beşiktaş - Şişli

47. Murat Karamancı Student Center
48. Zorlu Center
49. Haaz Gallery
50. Cemil Topuzlu Open-Air Theatre
51. Vodafone Park
52. Istanbul Naval Museum
53. Beşiktaş Fish market
54. Esma Sultan Mansion
55. Taut House
56. July 15th Martyrs Bridge (Bosphorus Bridge)

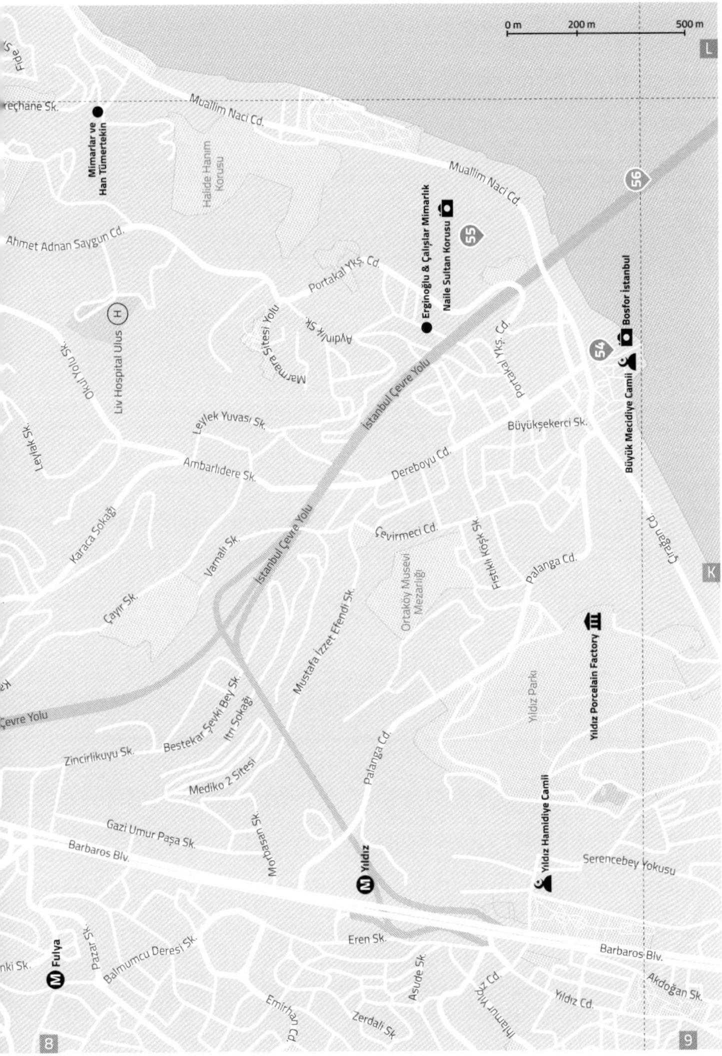
0 m
200 m
500 m
L
K
8
9
Mimarlar ve Han Tümertekin
Muallim Naci Cd.
Halide Hanım Korusu
Erginoğlu & Çalışlar Mimarlık
Naile Sultan Korusu
55
56
54
Bosfor İstanbul
Büyük Mecidiye Camii
Ahmet Adnan Saygun Cd.
Portakal Ykş. Cd.
Liv Hospital Ulus
Okul Yolu Sk.
Marmara Sitesi Yolu
Aydınlık Sk.
İstanbul Çevre Yolu
Leylek Yuvası Sk.
Leylak Sk.
Büyükşekerci Sk.
Dereboyu Cd.
Ambarlıdere Sk.
Karaca Sokağı
Çevirmeci Cd.
Fıstıklı Köşk Sk.
Çırağan Cd.
Varnalı Sk.
Palanga Cd.
Ortaköy Musevi Mezarlığı
Çayır Sk.
Mustafa İzzet Efendi Sk.
Yıldız Porcelain Factory
Yıldız Parkı
Bestekar Şevki Bey Sk.
Itri Sokağı
Çevre Yolu
Zincirlikuyu Sk.
Mediko 2 Sitesi
Yıldız Hamidiye Camii
Gazi Umur Paşa Sk.
Barbaros Blv.
Morbasan Sk.
Serencebey Yokusu
Yıldız
Eren Sk.
Fulya
Pazar Sk.
Balmumcu Deresi Sk.
Asude Sk.
Ihlamur Yıldız Cd.
Yıldız Cd.
Akdoğan Sk.
Emirhan Cd.
Zerdali Sk.

38. Now Bomonti

Cumhuriyet, Yeniyol Sk. No:2
34380 Şişli, Istanbul

partially open to the public
+90 212 334 22 00
info@nowbomonti.com.tr
nowbomonti.com.tr

M2 > Osmanbey

37T, 38KT, 48T, 49T, 50L, 55B, AVR3K > Bomonti-Tünel
70FE, 70FY, AVR3K > Ortanca

The Now Bomonti office tower, designed by Tabanlıoğlu Architects in 2018, is located in the Şişli district, one of the areas in the city centre undergoing widespread renewal. The 16 storey building is a parallelepiped entirely faced in sheer glass. Each facade resembles a glass sculpture: entire sections of glass wall are recessed back from the roof eave line to create external walkways and balconies that connect various office spaces, for the exclusive use of employees. This play of recessed spaces generates elegant movement, creating facades with striking impact. The void space system is also repeated within the building where certain areas with double height ceilings have been designed as indoor patios with planted gardens. With the Now Bomonti project, Tabanlıoğlu Architects have made a strong and important contribution to the architectural lexicon of the Şişli district, which is in full expansion.

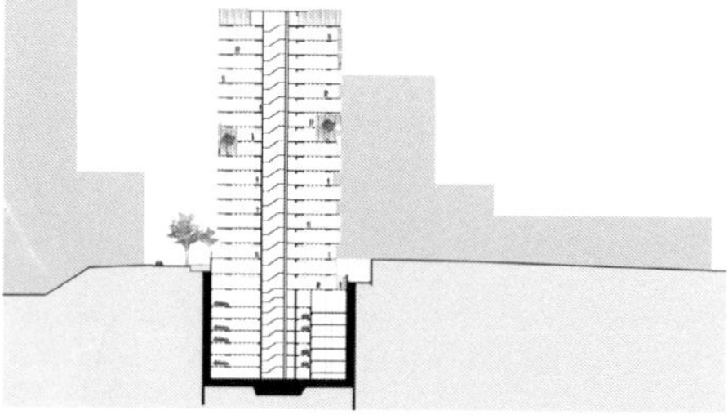

© Tabanlıoğlu Architects

architects
Tabanlıoğlu Architects

type
offices

construction
2018

39. Alt art space

Merkez Mah. Silahşör Cad. Birahane Sok. Tarihi Bomonti Bira Fabrikası No: 1
34384 Şişli, Istanbul

The - Sun / 1 pm - 9 pm
+90 212 296 29 29

M8 > Ayşekadın

B1 > Suadlye

37T, 38KT, 48T, 49T, 50L, 55B, AVR3K > Bomonti-Tünel
70FE, 70FY, AVR3K > Ortanca

After 2000, the Bomonti quarter underwent a rapid evolution in what it offered as a tourist attraction with the creation of new spaces designed to encourage social gathering. The centre of these new attractions was the area surrounding the open spaces of a famous brewery founded back in 1890. Already between 1930 and 1950, the area housed a German inspired beer garden. Following the opening of a number of luxury hotels, it was decided to convert the whole brewery area, creating a range of new functions. In 2015, the area was given the name "Bomonitada", designed to become "a cultural and entertainment space". The area now houses new restaurants, cafés, concert spaces and new buildings for cultural use. ŞANALarc carried out the project to create the Alt Art Space, a building designed for visual and performance arts, converted from one of the pavilions of the former brewery. The project was aimed at dividing the internal space of the existing structure in a flexible manner by carving out three different areas for two purposes: service and exhibition spaces that are interconnected with one another.

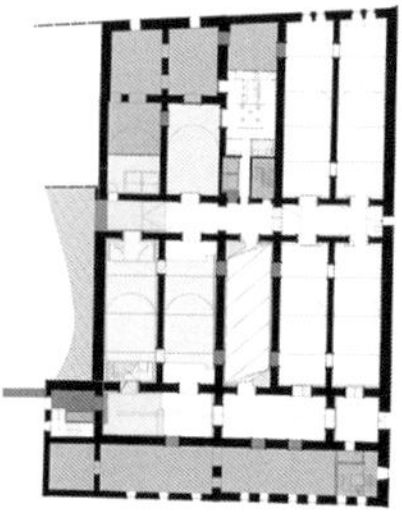

© ŞANALarc

architects
ŞANALarc

type
exhibition space

construction
2016

40. Trump Cadde

Kuștepe Mah. Mecidiyeköy Yolu Caddesi No:12 Trump Towers AVM BB / Zk03-Zk07b, Mecidiyeköy
34381 Șișli, Istanbul

open to the public
+ 90 212 3487840
avminfo@trumpistanbul.com.tr
www.trumpalisverismerkezi.com/trump-cadde

M7 > Mecidiyeköy

34, 34A, 34AS, 34BZ, 34G > Mecidiyeköy
Șișli-Yahya Kemal > Karkusuyu Sokak
Atakan Sokak > Șișli - Yahya Kemal

The Trump Cadde complex, designed by GAD Architecture in 2014, is far more than what you might expect from a standard shopping mall. It is based on the concept of the traditional bazaar, and is built from shipping containers placed on top of one another, where open spaces like small squares and plazas alternate with enclosed areas and other zones protected by projecting elements. Main alleys cross each other, slicing through the "bazaar" and forming a system of internal horizontal connections. Stores and restaurants intersect in a dense assortment of spaces on two levels to recreate a modern version of the traditional Ottoman urban fabric. A vibrant blend of colours and materials add to the atmosphere, providing new and unusual glimpses in a relatively limited space. The overall impression is one of an eclectic and unique complex with an unconventional twist.

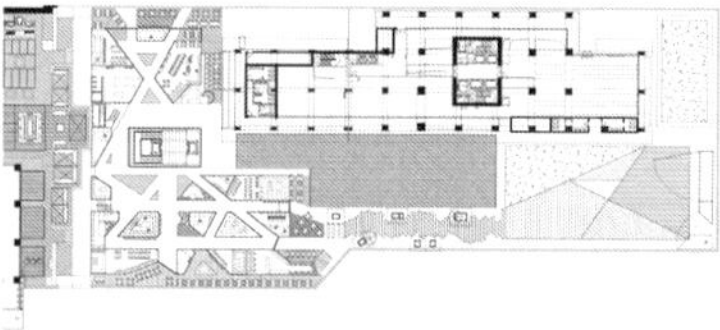

architects
GAD Architecture

type
commercial centre

construction
2014

41. Loft Gardens

Esentepe, Oto Çk. No:4
34394 Şişli, Istanbul

partially open to the public

M2, M6 > Levent

29B > Levent Metro
Bacadibi (bus station)
Fabrikalar (bus station)

Loft Gardens is a 21 floor loft apartment building designed by Tabanlioğlu Architects, inspired by the model of its twin building, Levent Loft. The basic design concept is aimed at creating buildings that represent an extension of residential architecture and contemporary urban lifestyle. The glass facade is composed of solid surfaces and voids as well as projecting elements that form balconies, giving the facade a vibrant dynamic effect. The building is completed with a contemporary pronaos: an extension of the building's steel structure that forms a cage surrounding the top floor, recessed from the main facade. The building contains loft apartments of various heights and surface areas, internal gardens and balconies. All windows are full height, flooding the interiors with natural light, making the apartments seem larger and full of light.

© Hélène Binet

architects
Tabanlıoğlu Architects

type
residential

construction
2010

42. Tekfen Tower

Esentepe, 4. Levent Kavşağı No:209
34394 Şişli, Istanbul

partially open to the public
+90 212 357 00 00
services-info@tekfen.com.tr
www.tekfenservices.com

M2, M6 > Levent

29B > Levent Metro
Bacadibi (bus station)
Fabrikalar (bus station)

Tekfen Tower was built by Tekfen Holding, and designed by Swanke Hayden Connell Architects. Construction began in 1999 and was completed in 2003. The skyscraper stands in the 4th Levent district on the European side of the city, one of the main business districts in Istanbul, home to a large number of major international business headquarters. Externally, the Tekfen Tower is composed of a single block; parts of the facade are glass walled and others are clad with red panels to create a distinctive pattern. At the top of the building, the facade of the last two floors is clad in white panels. The Tekfen Tower building has 26 floors, and is 117.5 metres tall. The internal surface area covers 33,000 square metres. The internal decor features large light-filled spaces creating a comfortable and pleasant work environment.

architects
Swanke Hayden Connell Architects

type
offices

construction
2002

43. Levent Loft

Esentepe,
Büyükdere Cd. No:201
34394 Şişli, Istanbul

partially open to the public

M2, M6 > Levent

29B > Levent Metro
Bacadibi (bus station)
Fabrikalar (bus station)

This residential building was formerly an office block in the Şişli district. Tabanlıoğlu Architects reconverted the building, creating fashionable, high-quality loft apartments in a zone that has attracted renewed interest following its recent development as a new dynamic business centre. The site of this intervention is adjacent to a factory: a green space was planted in the division between the two buildings, a Zen garden that separates the functional areas within the site itself. The apartments were built inside the reinforced concrete framework, with free access to the common meeting places, pool and social recreational areas. The loft modules vary in size and style, ranging between 68 and 182 square metres, based on a duplex-style layout. Each individual unit can be identified in the facade through the play of projecting glazed bays, each one different in size and shape, and through the variation in geometrical composition created by the different recessed private terraces.

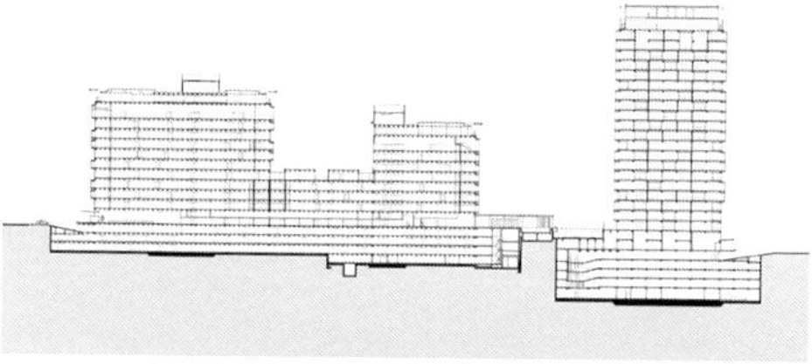

architects
Tabanlıoğlu Architects

type
residential

construction
2007

44. Zorlu Levent

Büyükdere Caddesi
No:199, Levent 199
34330 Şişli, Istanbul

partially open to the public

M2, M6 > Levent

29B > Levent Metro
Bacadibi (bus station)
Fabrikalar (bus station)

In the heart of the financial district, more precisely on Büyükdere Caddesi, stands a 170 metre office tower designed by Tabanlioglu Architects. The tower is part of a complex including other low-rise buildings connected to one another with bridges and walkways. The two and four storey block constructed along Talatpaşa Caddesi houses garden-offices, and the different buildings that surround the high-rise tower at ground level are landscaped with roof gardens. At street level, the spaces created by the juxtaposition of the taller and lower buildings form a series of public courtyards and areas designed for social gathering. The 41 storey tower is exclusively dedicated to office space, while the lower-rise buildings, including the covered areas inside the complex at street level, have been designed for retail shopping stores.

architects
Tabanlıoğlu Architects

type
offices

construction
2014

45. Kanyon

Esentepe Mahallesi,
Büyükdere Cd. No:185
34394 Şişli, Istanbul

Mon - Sun / 10 am - 10 pm
+90 212 317 53 30
bilgi@kanyon.com.tr
www.kanyon.com.tr

M2, M6 > Levent

Bacadibi (bus station)
Fabrikalar (bus station)

The Kanyon, designed by the Tabanlioğlu Architects and Jerde Partnership in 2006, is one of the largest residential, retail, and business complexes in Europe. All functions of daily life are concentrated within the complex, introducing a new concept in urban life. The complex was conceived as an organic structure, featuring fluid sinuous shapes that surround a perfect element: a quarter sphere, that forms the heart of the structure. The exterior of the spherical element has a hollowed void, like a cave, which contains a performing stage. This element is connected to the rest of the structure by suspended pedestrian walkways. As with natural rock, the external profile of the sphere is not linear: projecting and recessed sections alternate in perfect harmony between the levels above and below, a dynamic space that engages the public. Strolling around the ground floor, looking up, the public has the feeling of crossing a rift between two rocky walls of Antelope Canyon. The residential and office towers with their curving shapes and planted green gardens, are the tallest buildings in the complex.

architects
Tabanlıoğlu Architects,
Jerde Partnership

type
commercial centre

construction
2006

46. Demir Demirgil Theatre Hall

Bebek, Boğaziçi University, Öğrenci Faaliyetleri Binası
34342 Beşiktaş, Istanbul

open to the public

M6 > Boğaziçi Üniversitesi İstasyonu

59RK > Boğaziçi Üniversitesi Kampüsü
43R, 59R, 59RH, 59RS, 559C > Boğaziçi Üniversitesi
22, 22RE, 29D, 40, 40T > Aşiyan

F4 > Aşiyan

Aşiyan-Anadolu Hisarı-Küçüksu, Üsküdar-Aşiyan > Aşiyan

The Boğaziçi University is located in the vibrant historic Beşiktaş district overlooking the Bosphorus. One of the buildings belonging to the university complex is the Demir Demirgil Salonu theatre, which has existed on campus since 1920, and which required restoration to provide functional and performance upgrading. The improvement and renovation project was assigned to Halukar Architecture. The aim was to improve the visibility, access, and acoustics in the theatre hall with carefully focused interventions that would upgrade the theatre to current standards without compromising the former historical characteristics. The theatre measures 450 square metres. All wall cladding and plaster false ceilings were removed revealing the original wooden A-frame structure that had supported the former ceiling. The longitudinal section of the hall was transformed, raising the height of the audience stalls opposite the stage, creating seating for 176 people, and optimising viewing capacity for spectators. The perimeter walls were clad with a type of refractory brick to improve the acoustic quality. Halükar Architecture also renovated the technical services necessary for theatrical performances: lighting and sound systems were installed between the wooden A-frame beams, and the backstage areas were completely redesigned to create a more efficient and convenient space layout.

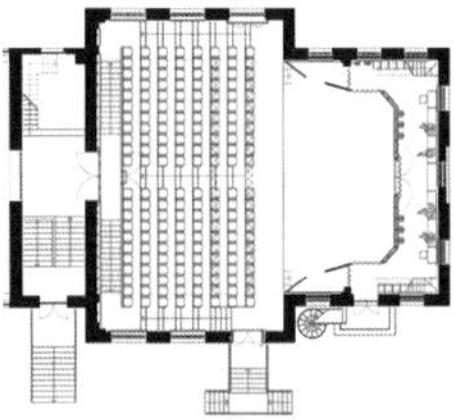

architects
Halükar Architecture

type
theatre

construction
1920

47. Murat Karamancı Student Center

Arnavutköy,
Kuruçeşme Cd. No:87
34345 Beşiktaş, Istanbul

open to the public
+90 212 3592222
website.robcol.k12.tr

57UL > Şehit Hüseyin Tunç

The Murat Karamanci Student Center, designed by the Ahmet Alataş Workshop, was built inside the complex of one of the oldest American schools in Istanbul, Robert College, built in 1863. The school needed a much larger space for its dining hall, but historical and landscape limitations linked with the college made it impossible to build a new structure. The architects decided to transform the old college gym by creating a vaulted hangar-like structure with a steel frame; it was covered with steel mesh and a membrane to provide a large, light-filled, open space. The intervention focused on reinforcing the structure and replacing the former membrane with a more efficient translucent material, and redesigning the internal layout with a double height mezzanine floor. Another important element is the interaction between the structure and its surroundings. Trees and shrubs do not only surround the building, but have been planted inside the structure, eliminating the effect of an artificial threshold and creating a direct contact between man and nature.

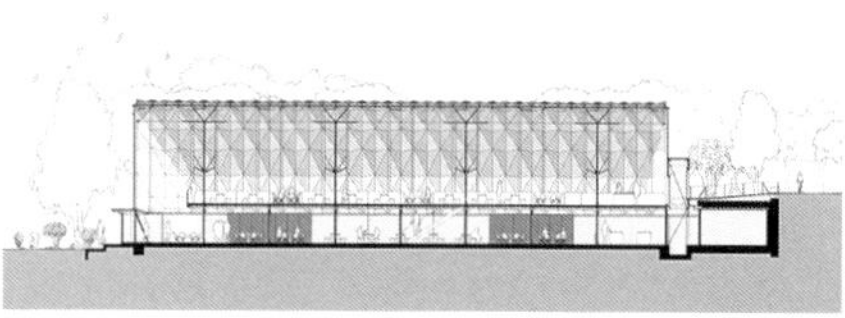

© Ahmet Alataş Workshop

architects
Ahmet Alataş Workshop

type
school

construction
1863 / 2016

48. Zorlu Center

Levazım Mahallesi,
Koru Sokak No:2
34340 Beşiktaş, Istanbul

Mon - Sun / 10 am - 10 pm
+90 212 9 9240124
www.zorlucenter.com

M2 > Gayrettepe

Zincirlikuyu Metrobüs
(bus station)

The Zorlu Center, designed by EAA – Emre Arolat Architecture and Tabanlıoğlu Architects, was built in 2013 in the Beşiktaş district, on the European side of the city. The project was designed based on a topographical analysis and an interpretation of the geographical site. The shopping centre is composed of four towers that rise from a base structure with an organic shape; two large steep arms, like two hills, enclose the retail stores and an auditorium. These two arms are composed of a series of staggered levels to create green planted terraced areas. Between the two arms is a large internal plaza designed as a meeting place for socialising, but mainly as the initial entrance to the complex that is crossed by the public. All spaces in the Zorlu Center follow the same principle, a continuous connection between interior and exterior, private and public spaces. Each area is connected with others in an open fluid way to form a flexible and innovative environment.

© EAA – Emre Arolat Architecture

architects
EAA – Emre Arolat Architecture, Tabanlıoğlu Architects

type
commercial centre

construction
2013

49. Haaz Gallery

Harbiye Mah. Teşvikiye Cad. No:3-B Güneş Apt. D:1, Teşvikiye
34000 Şişli, Istanbul

Mon - Fri / 9 am - 6 pm
+90 212 230 9600
info@haaz.info
www.haaz.info

M2 > Osmanbey Metro Station

BŞK/1, D53 > Teşvikiye
D46 >Nişantaşı

In 2010, GAD Architecture carried out a renovation project to redesign the exhibition space of the Haaz Gallery in the popular shopping district of Teşvikiye. The retail and exhibition space covers an area of more than 200 square metres spread over two floors. The main aim was to create an exhibition space with maximum flexibility; using carefully selected materials, the architects wanted to provide a welcoming comfortable atmosphere, closer to the feeling of a private home than a retail space. This is obvious in the choice of wood (for the herring bone parquet flooring) and stone, both of which are popular materials used in the construction of traditional Turkish homes. The external facade features a series of black steel tubes combined with led lighting to attract passers-by. Once visitors enter the ground floor, they find 5 wide steps that are also used to expand the interior decor presentation space and act as further exhibition space to display the objects on show.

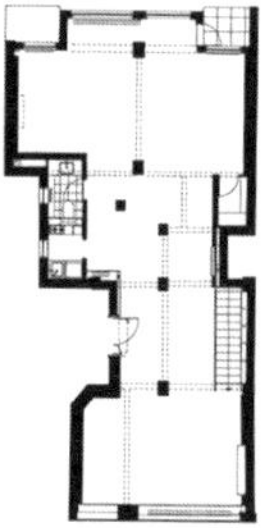

architects
GAD Architecture

type
art gallery

construction
2010

50. Cemil Topuzlu Open-Air Theatre

Harbiye Mahallesi,
Taşkışla Cd. No:8
34367 Şişli, Istanbul

open to the public
+90 212 2321652

BŞK/1, D53 > Cemil Topuzlu Açık Hava Tiyatrosu
Harbiye Askeri Müze (bus station)

The open-air theatre, also known as Açıkhava Tiyatrosu, is located in the Şişli district. The original proposal for this open-air theatre was based on a project by the French urban planner, Henri Prost, in the 1930s. However, the inauguration was not held until 1947, the result of a combined project designed by the architects, Nihad Yucel and Nahid Uysal. The structure was later modified for stage production requirements by Carl Ebert, director of the Ankara State Conservatory who did not finish the upgrading project until the 1950s. It was inaugurated with the performance of the Greek tragedy, Oedipus Rex by Sophocles. Great attention was paid to the choice of construction materials. The variations in the stone facade colour recall the traditional building style of the area: it is a narrative in limestone rich in fossils combined with stone from Uzunköprü, an Asian city situated in the Edirne province. The structure is clearly based on the large-scale classical Greek theatre model. The semi-circular tier seating has a capacity for 3,972 spectators, and the orchestra section can accommodate 80 musicians, while the vast stage area is able to contain at least 300 actors and supporting cast.

architects
Nihad Yucel, Nahid Uysal

type
theatre

construction
1946

51. Vodafone Park

Vişnezade Mahallesi, Kadırgalar Cd. No:1
34330 Beşiktaş, Istanbul

Tue - Sun / 10 am - 6 pm
+90 212 9481903

Vodafone Park, designed by DB Architecture, is located in the Beşiktaş district and was built on the site of the former BJK İnönü stadium designed by the Italian architect, Paolo Vietti-Violi. The design had to respect three fundamental aspects: the stadium architecture had to reflect the history, heritage and community of the city. In fact, the stadium's vicinity to the Dolmabahçe Palace [Dolmabahçe Sarayı], clock tower and mosque, imposed a Classical architectural style linked with the history of Istanbul. The new design has a perfectly symmetrical elliptical shape based on the form of the old stadium. The exterior is surrounded by a monumental colonnade based on the trilithon structure recalling ancient Classical architecture. The new elliptical stadium has completely preserved and incorporated the old iron Marathon gate and towers that closed the former stadium. This impressive structure forms a link between the sea and the hinterland of Istanbul. It is roofed with a reticular structure topped with a white canopy cover.

Dolmabahçe Palace (bus station) **37T, 38KT, 48T, 49T, 49Z, 50L, 55B, 62G** > Dolmabahçe-Tünel

T1 > Kabataş Tramvay istasyonu

Beşiktaş-Adalar, Üsküdar-Kabataş > Kabataş

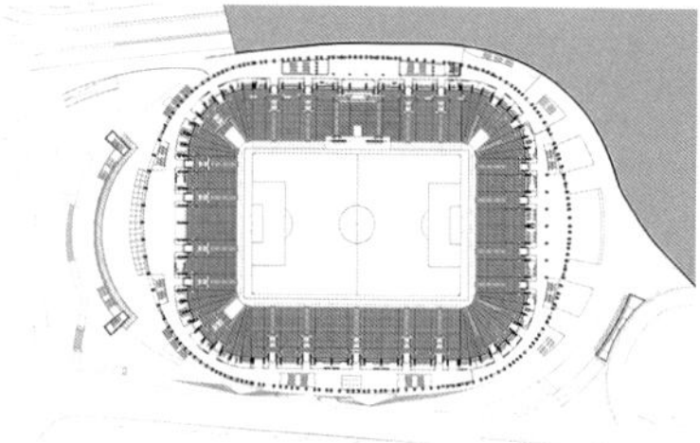

© DB Architecture

architects
DB Architecture

type
stadium

construction
2016

52. Istanbul Naval Museum

Sinanpaşa,
Beşiktaş Cd. No:6 D:1
34353 Beşiktaş, Istanbul

Tue - Fri / 9 am - 5 pm
Sat - Sun / 10 am - 6 pm
+90 212 327 43 45
muze.istanbul.iletisim@dzkk.tsk.tr
denizmuzesi.dzkk.tsk.tr

A national competition was launched in 2004 for the design of the Istanbul Naval Museum [Deniz Müzesi]. Architects were requested to propose a new exhibition project, while conserving the style of the original building dating back to the 1940s. The winning project was presented by Teğet, which completed the construction ready for the public opening in 2013. The project focused particular attention on the organisation of the exhibition space for the permanent boat gallery. It was designed as a single space so that visitors are able to view the whole collection at the same time. The boats are positioned parallel with one another, with the sterns facing the Bosphorus. This influenced the innovative design of the facade facing the sea: each boat has a corresponding vertical element in the facade, thus creating a series of solid and transparent sections. The large exhibition space is crossed by seven steel overhead bridges that allow visitors to also observe the exhibition from above. The Naval Museum is the first contemporary building to be constructed on the banks of the Bosphorus.

121CS, BŞK/1, TB2 > Naval Museum
BŞK/1, BŞK/5, SRY-14, SRY-16 > Beşiktaş

Adalar-Beşiktaş, Beşiktaş-Kabataş-Karaköy-Kasımpaşa-Sütlüce-Eyüp, Boğaz Hattı, Kadıköy-Sarıyer, Küçüksu-Beşiktaş-Kabataş, Rumeli Kavağı-Eminönü, Uzun Boğaz Turu > Beşiktaş Iskelesi

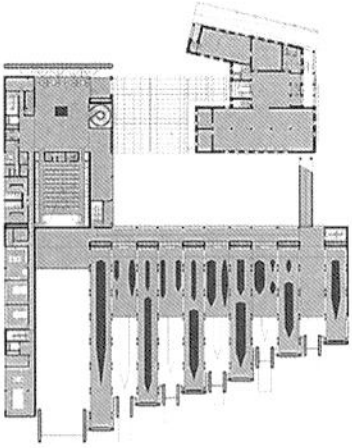

architects
Teğet

type
museum

construction
2010

53. Beşiktaş Fish market

Sinanpaşa Mahallesi, Mumcu Bakka Sk.
34353 Beşiktaş, Istanbul

Mon - Sun / 8 am - 9 pm

Beşiktaş Durak (bus station)
121CS, D61 > Beşiktaş Bazaar
BŞK/2, D31, D36, D61, D62 > Akaretler

This project is composed of a limited space nestled below a concrete shell. It was the new concept for the Beşiktaş Fish market [Beşiktaş Balık Pazarı] designed by GAD Architecture in 2010 in the local Beşiktaş quarter. The aim of the project was to differentiate the fish market activities from the pedestrian traffic in the square while not separating them completely. The fish market is conveniently located in the centre of the public space, leaving easy free traffic flow around the perimeters. The triangular site inspired the structure that is composed of a single triangular roof, whose apexes curve downwards to form the support elements for the vaulted roof. The free internal space for the fish market activities covers a surface of about 350 square metres. Clearly, this project was based on a very simple concept: that of taking a bi-dimensional surface and modelling it to become a complex three-dimensional structure. An interesting system of single lights hangs from the vaulted ceiling intrados over the fish stall counters. At street level, low walls around the perimeter, decorated with coloured majolica mosaics, conceal the technical equipment necessary for retail markets.

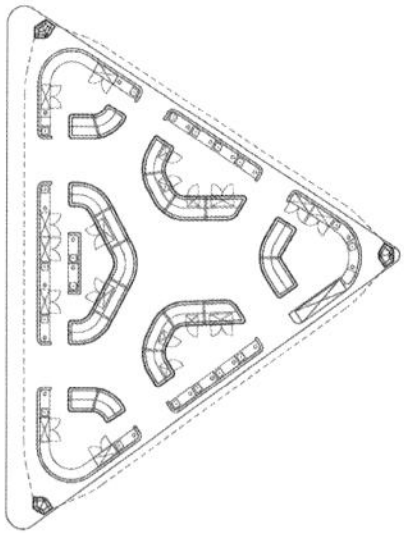

© GAD Architecture

architects
GAD Architecture

type
market

construction
2009

54. Esma Sultan Mansion

Ortaköy, Mecidiye Köprüsü Sk. No:1
34347 Beşiktaş, Istanbul

open to the public

esmasultan-info@themarmarahotels.com
www.themarmarahotels.com/esma-sultan

Ortaköy-Kabataş Erkek Lisesi (bus station)
Ortaköy (bus station)

Boğaz Hattı, Ortaköy-Üsküdar-Kadıköy, Rumeli Kavağı-Eminönü > Ortaköy

This three storey brick building was the former residence of the Princess Esma Sultan. It was designed by the architect Sarkis Balyan in 1875, but was later destroyed by fire in 1975, leaving only the external walls intact. In 2001, the GAD Architecture firm was commissioned to reconstruct the building to create a multi-function space for events and exhibitions, while preserving the pre-existing brick structure, and limiting intervention to the interior. It is a "building within a building", designed to create a process of architectural stratification with different layers of styles and materials. These combine to produce an extremely rich and complex effect. The intervention involved erecting a steel and glass structure within the walls, an effect designed to enchant those who enter the building. Visitors are fascinated by the beauty of the ruins and the history of a bygone era, suspended in time between the past and present.

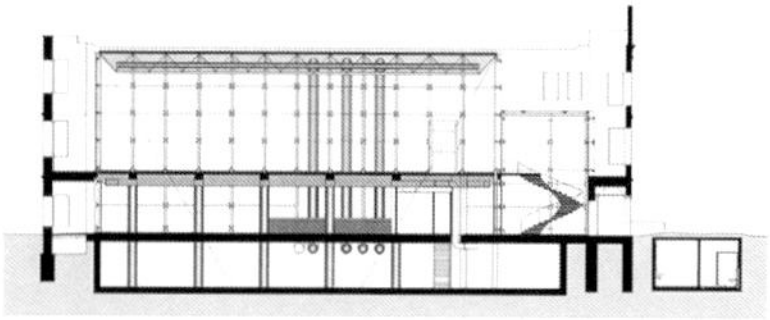

architects
Sarkis Balyan /
GAD Architecture

type
multi-purpose building

construction
1875 / 2002

55. Taut House

Ortaköy, Emin Vafi Korusu 61E
34347 Beşiktaş, Istanbul

external viewing only

Ortaköy-Kabataş Erkek Lisesi (bus station)
Ortaköy (bus station)

Boğaz Hattı, Ortaköy-Üsküdar-Kadıköy, Rumeli Kavağı-Eminönü > Ortaköy

Bruno Taut's house [Taut Evi] is located in the Ortaköy district, in the shadow of the pillars of the 15 Temmuz Şehitler Köprüsü Bridge. Bruno Taut had lived in Turkey since 1935 and had been involved in numerous other construction projects in the city. A year before his death, while still in exile in Turkey, in 1937, Bruno Taut decided to design his own home on an open site with a view over the Bosphorus canal. The topography of the site in question was rather complex: the problem of the steep slope and strong difference in quota between the higher terrain and the lower part towards the shoreline was resolved with a concrete structure composed of two tall slender stilts able to support the main fabric of the house on a level with the street. The house is partly suspended, and partly anchored to the terrain. As is clearly visible, the concept incorporates elements from Japanese Pagoda design (evident in the construction of the suspended octagonal living area) and traditional Ottoman house or *yali* architecture. A small winding staircase leads from the irregular octagonal living space up to the architect's private studio: a contained intimate space, also octagonal, with glass walls and a traditional Turkish pavilion hipped roof.

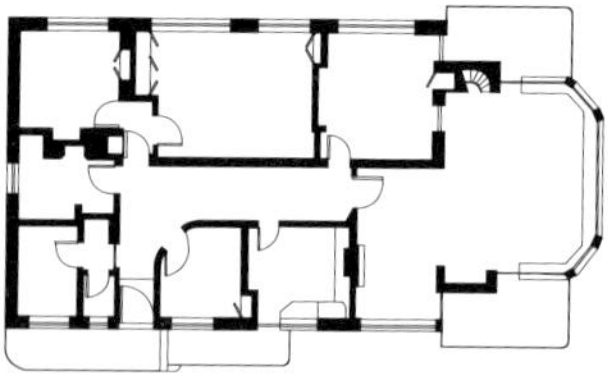

architects
Bruno Taut

type
residential building

construction
1938

56. July 15th Martyrs Bridge (Bosphorus Bridge)

Kuzguncuk, 15 Temmuz Şehitler Köprüsü
34000 Üsküdar, Istanbul

open to the public

22, 22B, 22RE, 40, 40T, BŞK/5 > Ortaköy
C118, D24, Üsküdar-Rasathane > Abdullahağa Caddesi

Anadolu Kavağı-Üsküdar, Boğaz Hattı > Beylerbeyi
Boğaz Hattı, Ortaköy-Üsküdar-Kadıköy, Rumeli Kavağı-Eminönü > Ortaköy

The July 15th Martyrs Bridge [15 Temmuz Şehitler Köprüsü] was one of the first suspended bridges to be built over the Bosphorus, connecting the two parts of Istanbul, linking Europe with Asia. Designed by the British engineers, Gilbert Roberts and William Brown, it was opened in 1973 to celebrate the 50th anniversary of the foundation of the Turkish Republic. The structure is 1,560 metres long and is suspended with steel stays and suspension cables from two towers, one at each end of the bridge. The deck has 6 traffic lanes in the centre and pedestrian walkways on each side. When it was designed and built, the July 5th Martyrs Bridge was considered one of the most innovative in the world because of its construction technology and still today, represents an important traffic hub and for the link between both sides of the Bosphorus.

architects
Sir Gilbert Roberts,
William Brown

type
infrastructure

construction
1970 / 1973

0 m
100 m
250 m
Mavi Sk.
Şeyh Şamil Sk.
Neşet Bey Sk.
Neşet Bey Sk.
Neşet Bey Sk.
Kağıtcıbaşı Sk.
Bakkalbaşı Sk.
Bahçe Sk.
Kağıtcıbaşı Sk.
Yapı Merkezi
58
Atilla Sk.
Şile Otoyolu
Millet Parkı
Kısıklı Cd.
Gülerce Sk.
Resmi Efendi Sk.
Tunuslu Mahmut Paşa Cd.
Hacı Reşitpaşa Sokağı
59
Burhaniye Abdullahağa Cd.
İstanbul Çevre Yolu
İstanbul Çevre Yolu
İstanbul Çevre Yolu
Kısıklı Cd.
Kuşbakışı Cd.
Altunizade Kavş
L
Burhaniye Abdullahağa Cd.
Kuşbaşı Cd.
İnci Çk.
Mahir İz Cd.
Rasimağa Sk.
Oymacı Sk.
Studio Vertebra
57
Rasimağa Sk.
Kuşbakışı Cd.
Şht. Selman Kalender Sk.
Mercure Istanbul Altunizade
Kısıklı Cd.
Aka Gündüz Sk.
Oymacı Sk.
Gümüşyolu Cd.
Nakkaştepe Musevi Mezarlığı
Maruf Sk.
İmam Galip Sk.
İcadiye Bağlarbaşı Cd.
Haluk Türksoy Sok.
Tago Architects
Ayarcıbaşı Sk.
Arzu Ayaktar Sk.
Cemil Meriç Sk.
Sübyeci Sk.
Can Yücel Sk.
Kurtçelebi Sk.
Temaşa Sk.
Shibuya Cd.
Bağlarbaşı Rum Ortodoks Mezarlığı
G

Kadıköy - Üsküar - Ataşehir

57. Vakko Fashion Headquarters
58. İyzico
59. Doğan Holding Headquarters
60. Validebağ Konaklari Sales Office
61. Eurasia Tunnel – Operation & Maintenance Building
62. Apartman 18

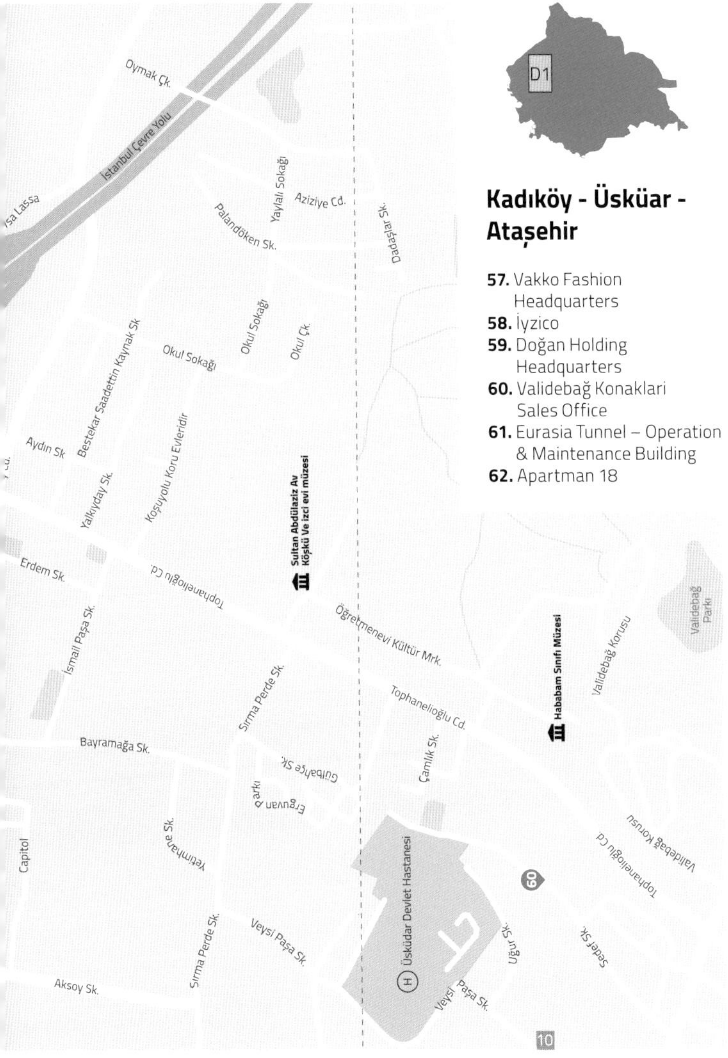

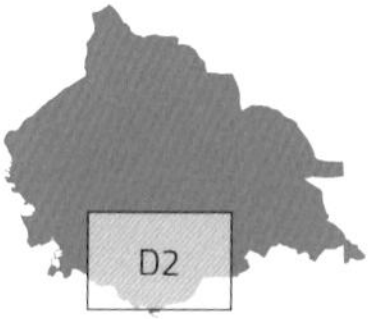

Kadıköy - Üsküar - Ataşehir

63. Bahriye Üçok Ecological Kindergarten
64. Mermerler Plaza Kozyatağı
65. Quick Tower
66. Ulugöl Otomotiv Office Building
67. Umur Printing and Stationery Factory
68. Yeşilvadi Mosque
69. Sur Yapi Offices

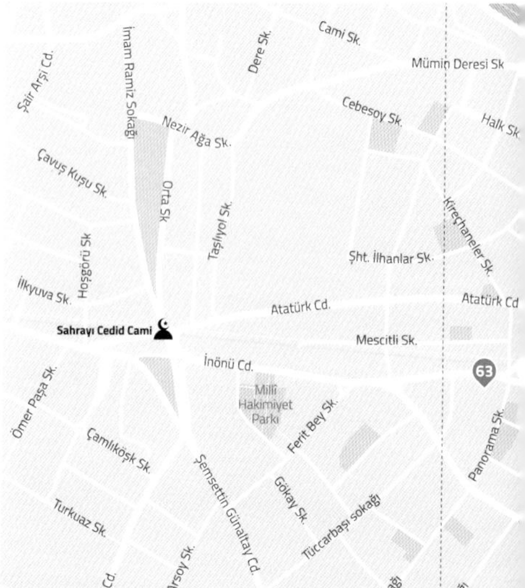

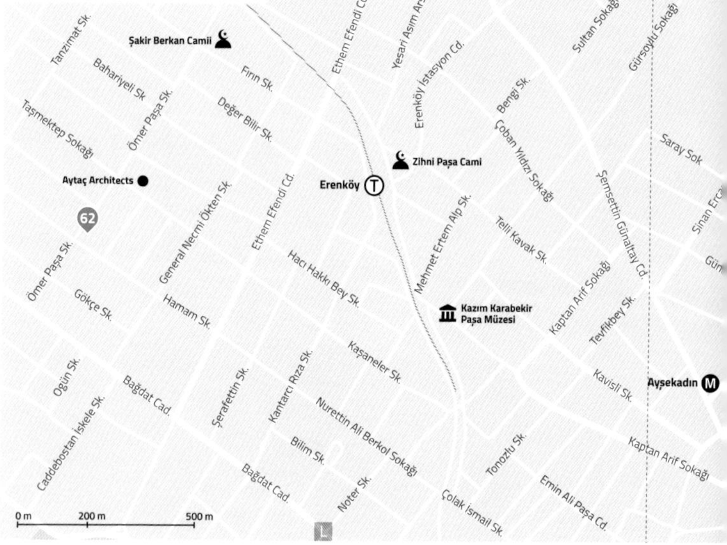

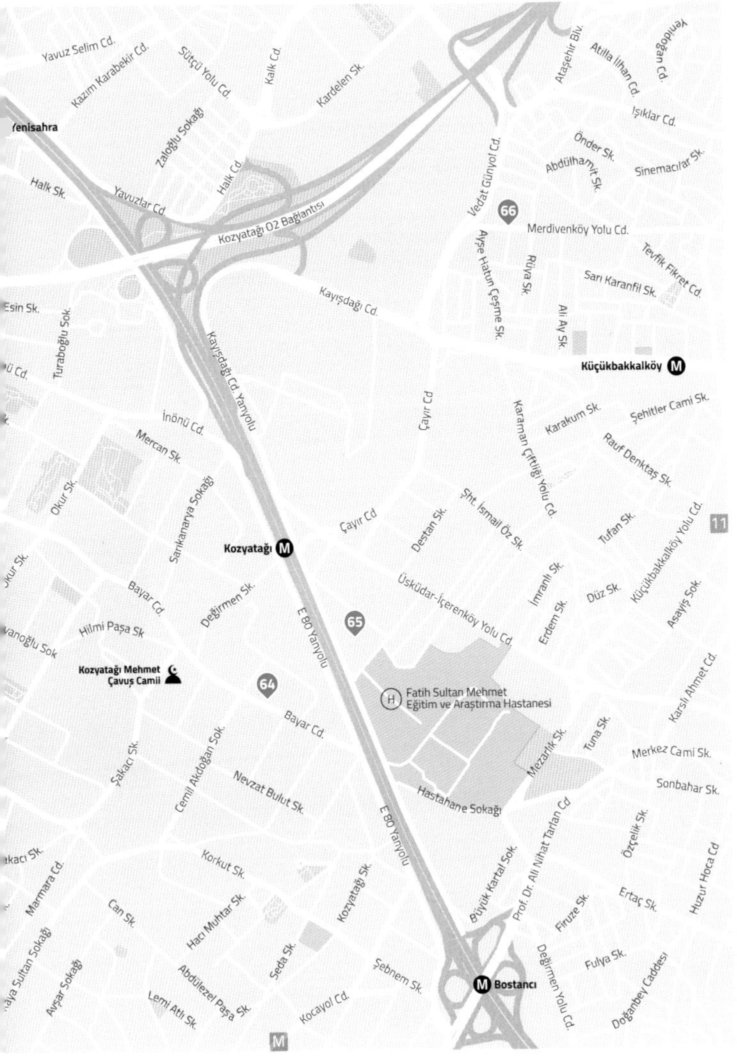
Yavuz Selim Cd.
Kazım Karabekir Cd.
Sütçü Yolu Cd.
Kalk Cd.
Kardelen Sk.
Ataşehir Blv.
Atilla İlhan Cd.
Yenidoğan Cd.
Işıklar Cd.
Zaloğlu Sokağı
Halk Cd.
Halk Sk.
Yavuzlar Cd.
Kozyatağı O2 Bağlantısı
Vedat Günyol Cd.
Önder Sk.
Abdülhamit Sk.
Sinemacılar Sk.
66
Merdivenköy Yolu Cd.
Ayşe Hatun Çeşme Sk.
Rüya Sk.
Tevfik Fikret Cd.
Sarı Karanfil Sk.
Kayışdağı Cd.
Ali Ay Sk.
Esin Sk.
Turaboğlu Sok.
Küçükbakkalköy
M
Kayışdağı Cd. Yanyolu
Çayır Cd
Karaman Çiftliği Yolu Cd.
Karakum Sk.
Şehitler Cami Sk.
İnönü Cd.
Mercan Sk.
Rauf Denktaş Sk.
Okur Sk.
Sarıkanarya Sokağı
Şht. İsmail Öz Sk.
Destan Sk.
Çayır Cd
Tufan Sk.
Küçükbakkalköy Yolu Cd.
11
Kozyatağı
Üsküdar-İçerenköy Yolu Cd.
İmranlı Sk.
Düz Sk.
Asayiş Sok.
Bayar Cd.
Değirmen Sk.
Erdem Sk.
Hilmi Paşa Sk
65
E 80 Yanyolu
Kozyatağı Mehmet Çavuş Camii
64
Karslı Ahmet Cd.
H
Fatih Sultan Mehmet Eğitim ve Araştırma Hastanesi
Bayar Cd.
Mezarlık Sk.
Tuna Sk.
Merkez Cami Sk.
Şakacı Sk.
Cemil Akdoğan Sok.
Nevzat Bulut Sk.
Sonbahar Sk.
Hastahane Sokağı
Prof. Dr. Ali Nihat Tarlan Cd.
Özçelik Sk.
E 80 Yanyolu
Marmara Cd.
Korkut Sk.
Büyük Kartal Sok.
Huzur Hoca Cd
Kozyatağı Sk.
Ertaç Sk.
Can Sk.
Hacı Muhtar Sk.
Firuze Sk.
Avşar Sokağı
Seda Sk.
Fulya Sk.
Şebnem Sk.
Değirmen Yolu Cd.
Doğanbey Caddesi
Abdülezel Paşa Sk.
Bostancı
Lemi Atlı Sk.
Kocayol Cd.
M

57. Vakko Fashion Headquarters

Altunizade Mahallesi, Kuşbakışı Cd. No:35
34662 Üsküdar, Istanbul

external viewing only

M5 > Altunizade

14M, 15F, 15U, D30 > Kazdal Cami
D30 > Kuşbakışı

The Vakko Fashion Headquarters [Vakko Moda Merkezi] was inaugurated in January 2010, and was the first foreign project created by the American architectural firm, REX. The structure houses the executive and creative design offices, a library, an auditorium, and showrooms. The building covers an area of 12,500 square metres built around a reinforced concrete frame. The layout is square, but despite the large size and severe form, the building appears light and airy because of its glass clad, steel mesh structure. The whole building is set on pillars to elevate it from the terrain, creating a free space at ground level and conveying a feeling of lightness. The intervention has been perfectly adapted to the pre-existing structure, granting the building new life and a contemporary public image.

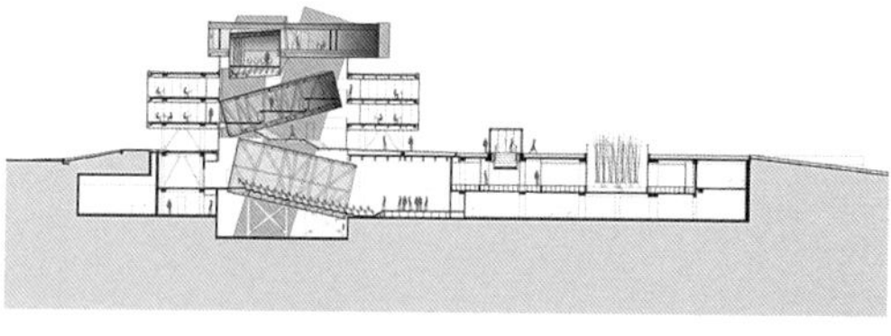

© REX

© Iwan Baan, courtesy REX, Architect

architects
REX

type
offices

construction
2010

58. İyzico

Burhaniye, Atilla Sk. No:7
34676 Üsküdar, Istanbul

external viewing only
+90 216 5990100
destek@iyzico.com

129T, 522, C56, C57, C66, C76, Kadıköy-Kirazlıtepe > Millet Bahçesi

The İyzico complex is located in a green planted area of about 6,000 square metres in Altunizade, and was designed in 2018 by the architectural firm, Ahmet Alataş Workshop. The objective was to improve the working conditions of the company employees, and aimed at increasing productivity and creativity in a calm serene atmosphere. The complex is composed of 4 buildings with different functions: a fitness area, meeting room, seminar space, staff cafeteria, offices, dining area and recreational space. The buildings are composed of a steel and glass structure with an extremely light and innovative appearance. The transparent effect of the structural elements also place employees in direct contact with the surrounding green space, creating a very relaxing work environment. The architectural design of the main block is composed of a cubic glass structure; attached to the rear is a translucent cylindrical element that houses the spiral staircase. The main facade is clad with metal mesh to provide shade inside the building and to create visual impact. The İyzico project has won several prizes for its technological innovation and the intelligent use of recyclable materials.

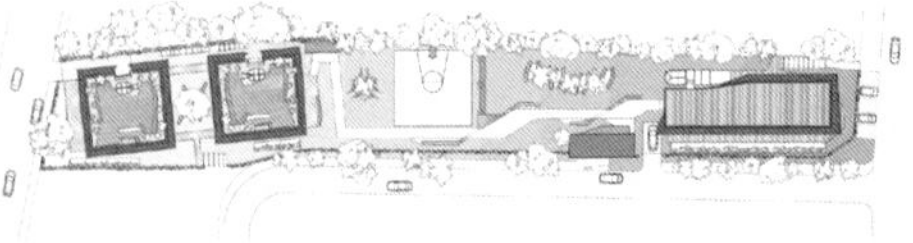

architects
Ahmet Alataş Workshop

type
offices

construction
2018

59. Doğan Holding Headquarters

Burhaniye,
Eski Kısıklı Cd. No:65
34676 Üsküdar, Istanbul

external viewing only
+90 216 5569000

www.doganholding.com.tr

M5 > Altunizade

129T, 522, C56, C57, C66, C76, Kadıköy-Kirazlıtepe > Millet Bahçesi

The Doğan Holding Headquarters building was designed by the NSMH architectural firm and was opened in 2011. The exterior is composed of a single rectangular block with a rather repetitive design. The facade design features plain simple elements, of pillars and cross-beams that create a kind of trilithic effect. The rectangular structure is built around a central courtyard, a large internal plaza where clients and employees can enjoy specifically designed relaxing spaces. In this area, large circular skylights provide natural light into the two underground floors of the building. There are three floors above ground. As can be seen in the cross-section, several double height areas house internal gardens and planted trees inside the building to provide different views of the greenery and to create a relaxing environment.

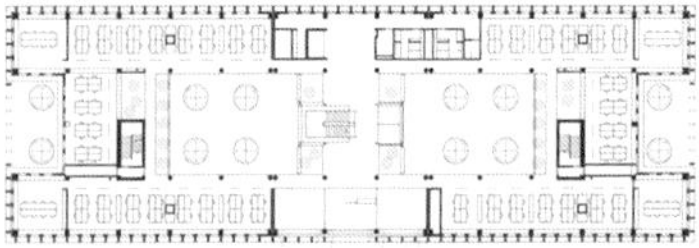

© NSMH

architects
NSMH

type
offices

construction
2011

60. Validebağ Konaklari Sales Office

Barbaros,
Tophanelioğlu Cd. No:72
34662 Üsküdar, Istanbul

partially open to the public
+90 216 4449327
info@dapyapi.com
www.dapyapi.com.tr/
validebag-konaklari

The Dap Construction Validebağ Konaklari Sales Office [Validebağ Konaklari Satis Ofisi] is located in the Üsküdar district in Istanbul. The building was designed by the architectural firm, Studio Vertebra, and was built in 2017. The design is based on a unique and expressive structure aimed at creating a building that would attract attention and would not pass unnoticed. For this reason the architects designed a tower with a surface area of 730 square metres, based on a steel structure, with a projecting steel and glass element on the top. The block contains spaces for various functions including the office spaces. Despite its size, the Validebağ Konaklari has a lightweight appearance, obtained through the use of semi-transparent coloured glazing on the three floor section exclusively dedicated to the stairs and elevators. The architectural design is particularly powerful and elegant in concept.

5, 11T, 12C, 14C, C57, C76 > Adile Sultan Kasrı

architects
Studio Vertebra

type
offices

construction
2017

61. Eurasia Tunnel – Operation & Maintenance Building

Selimiye, Dr. Eyüp Aksoy Cd. No:9
34662 Üsküdar, Istanbul

open to the public

bilgi@avrasyatuneli.com
www.avrasyatuneli.com

Harem Peron 3
(bus station)
BN1 > Çatladıkapı

With its construction, the double level Eurasia traffic tunnel [Avrasya Tüneli] connected the Asian and European sides of the Bosphorus for the first time. This infrastructure, designed by the Turkish company, Yapı Merkezi, covers a length of 14.6 kilometres, 3.4 kilometres of which are located about 106 metres below sea level. The project resolved the problem of traffic flow between the two continents. Opened in 2016, the tunnel is one of the most innovative and prestigious engineering projects in Turkey's history. Widely appreciated, not only by vehicle drivers, but also by international authorities for the comfort and safety it offers, this road tunnel has won a number of international prizes, including the Building Award of the Year in 2017 in the "Golden Category" by the Korean Society of Civil Engineers. The Eurasia Tunnel Operations & Maintenance Building [Avrasya Tüneli İşletme İnşaat ve Yatırım A.Ş.] is situated on the Asian side of Istanbul, and was designed by the London architectural firm, GMW Mimarlık, in 2014. It forms the nerve centre of the important infrastructural project of the Eurasia road tunnel. The rectangular, two storey super-structure is set on the same axis as the entrance to the tunnel. It is visible from all surrounding highways and is positioned above the maintenance structures built at ground level. The aim of this project was to create a contemporary building with strong architectural impact, while providing a pleasant comfortable work environment. One important aspect of the building design is the double skin facade: the outer skin is composed of perforated metal panels with a subtle wave pattern. At night, the external glazing transforms the building into an elegant glowing symbol of the Eurasia tunnel.

architects
GMW Mimarlık / Yapı Merkezi

type
infrastructure, offices

construction
2014 / 2016

62. Apartman 18

Erenköy, Ömer Paşa Sk. No:18
34730 Kadıköy, Istanbul

partially open to the public
+90 216 473 44 04

B1 > Erenköy

4, 16, 16D, D34, D38, ER2 > Caddebostan
GZ1 > Göztepe
ER2 > Taş Mektep

Apartman 18 is a project designed by the Aytaç Architects group in 2014. This luxury residential building is 10 storeys high and is located on the Asian side of the city. The architects wanted to pay homage to the vineyards of Erenköy that were destroyed to make way for the construction of densely built housing schemes in the area. The homage is realised through the stylised design of the building's facades recalling climbing vines. The opaque surface climbs in a zig-zag movement up the entire facade intersecting with the transparent glassed areas. The play between solids and voids, projecting and recessed spaces, and alternating materials gives the building an extremely contemporary quality, in sharp contrast with the surrounding urban context; its impact immediately captures the attention of passers-by. Apartman 18 has a roof garden which echoes and recalls the images of the vineyards that grew in this area in the past.

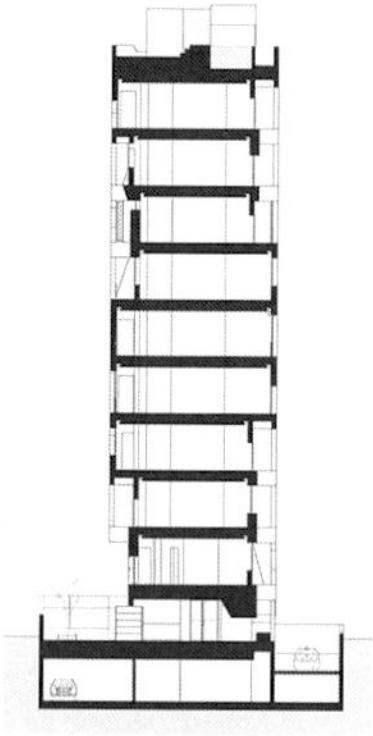

© Aytaç Architects

architects
Aytaç Architects

type
residential complex

construction
2014

63. Bahriye Üçok Ecological Kindergarten

Sahrayı Cedit,
İnönü Cd. No:36
34734 Kadıköy, Istanbul

partially open to the public
+90 216 3601145

cocukyuvalari.kadikoy.bel.tr/yuvalarimiz/bahriye-ucok-ekolojik-cocuk-yuvasi

C52, C116 > Panorama Sk
10B, C52 > Böcekli Camii

When the team of DİLEKCİ Architects (DDA) designed a ecological kindergarten in Kadıköy [Bahriye Üçok Ekolojik Çocuk Yuvası], in the Asian part of the city, they decided to focus the project on ecology, creating a prototype model of an "ecological nursery school" which was the first in Turkey. Every component, from the structure to the furnishings and the energy supplies, was researched in terms of environmental sustainability. Although the construction has a rather simple configuration, set around the central core containing common services, the internal layout was influenced by the desire to capture and utilise the thermal and chromatic properties of natural sunlight as far as possible. The roof resembles an origami sculpture, and is modelled like a series of "chimneys" topped with skylights which flood the interiors with natural daylight. The school has an internal surface area of 1,200 square metres, plus 1,600 square metres of outdoor garden and play area. Using Green Building principles, the concrete construction is covered with a green roof completely planted with meadow grass. In winter, the roofed space in the garden can be closed to absorb the sun's rays, to provide heating in the basement area through direct heat exchange.

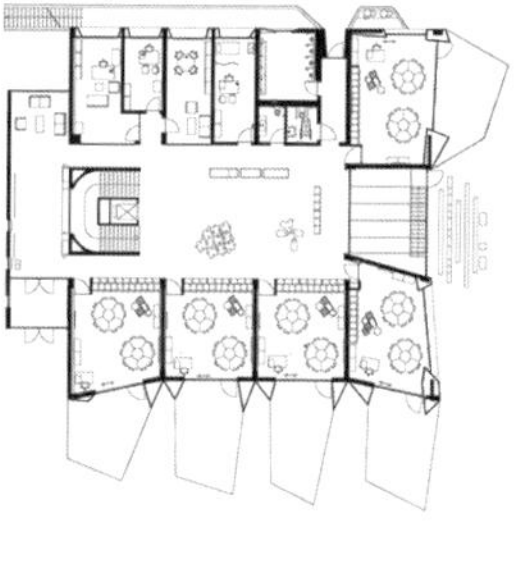

© DİLEKCİ Architects (DDA)

architects
DİLEKCİ Architects (DDA)

type
school

construction
2016

64. Mermerler Plaza Kozyatağı

Kozyatağı Mahallesi,
Bayar Cd. No:103
34742 Kadıköy, Istanbul

partially open to the public
+90 216 3066744

M4, M8 > Kozyatağı

19F > Fatih Sultan Mehmet Eğitim Ve Araştırma Hastanesi
10B, Kadıköy-Ataşehir, Kadıköy-Ferhatpaşa > Kozyatağı

Mermerler Plaza Kozyatağı, designed by the Ergün Mimarlık architecture team, was built in 2015 and is located in the Kozyatağı district of Istanbul. This office block is composed of two structures. The tower that forms the taller structure and the side fascia of the entire building are completely clad in undulating glass, while the north facade is clad in light grey composite stone. The tower is flanked by the second building that completes the complex. Like the tower, this building is clad in glass and microperforated mesh panels that act as sun-screens for the facade. The two buildings both feature balcony spaces designed as planted green areas where office employees can relax. The use of different materials provides an interesting contrast that enhances the architectural concept, giving it a more complex and diversified appearance.

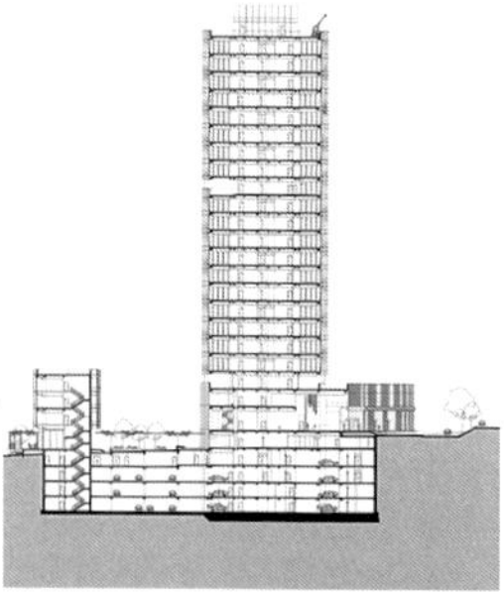

© Ergün Mimarlık

architects
Ergün Mimarlık

type
offices

construction
2015

65. Quick Tower

İçerenköy, Umut Sk. No:10-12
34752 Ataşehir, Istanbul

Mon - Sun / 8 am - 6 pm
+90 216 575 18 99
mhrgyo.com.tr/quick-tower

M4, M8 > Kozyatağı

In 2015, HPP Architects designed the office tower complex on a triangular site in the Ataşehir district in the southern part of the Asian area of the city. This building redefined the cityscape in what is considered the third financial district of Istanbul. As well as the underground car park that caters for more than seven hundred vehicles, the previously named AND tower [AND Kozyatağı], now called the Quick Tower, is composed of two connected structures: a central office block hub, containing the stairs and elevators, and a ground floor complex for assorted and retail space plus a conference hall.The total surface area is approximately 73,320 square metres, half of which is assigned to commercial activities and office space with 1,800 work places. At the foot of the tower, at ground level area between the new office block and Topçu İbrahim Sk., is an open square designed for public use. The steel frame tower facade has been clad with an unusual system: triangular aluminium louvre elements, set at different angles, create changing light and shadow effects according to the position of the sun during the day.

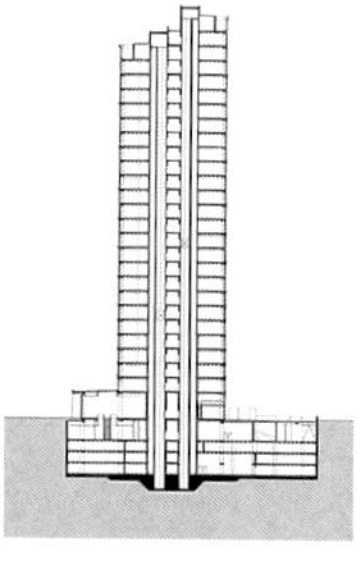

© HPP Architects

architects
HPP Architects

type
offices

construction
2015

66. Ulugöl Otomotiv Office Building

Küçükbakkalköy, Merdivenköy Yolu Cd. No:3
34758 Ataşehir, Istanbul

partially open to the public

M8 > Küçükbakkalköy

10A > Ataşehir Kaymakamlığı

The Ulugöl Otomotiv office building was built in 2013, and is located in the Ataşehir district in Istanbul. The project was designed by the architectural firm Tago Architects whose objective was to create a functional architectural design with a strong identity. This was realised with the construction of a building with 5 underground floors for garage space, and 11 floors above ground to house the offices. The facade of the building is composed of different blocks stacked on top of one another in irregular alignment in order to create a play of shadows and produce voids that contain planted terraces on various levels. The principle materials used for the construction are natural stone, glass and micro-perforated steel mesh. In order to create a decorative element on the facade, additional red aluminium panels have been used to clad the internal roofing of the planted terraces.

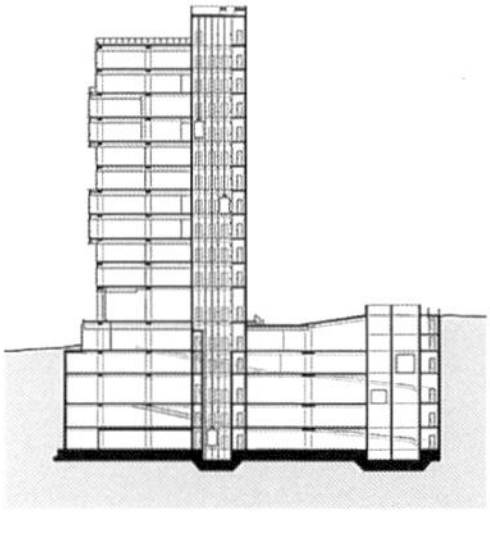

architects
Tago Architects

type
offices

construction
2013

67. Umur Printing and Stationery Factory

2. Cd. No:5
34775 Dudullu Osb,
Ümraniye, Istanbul

partially open to the public
+90 216 645 62 00
info@umur.com.tr
umurbasim.com

19A, 19E, 19EK, 19V, 131YS > Kadosan Sapağı

The initial project designed by architecture office NSMH for the Dudullu industrial area dates back to 15 years ago. Since then, the area has assumed a strategic role in the urban development of this part of the city, and the architects returned to work on this project with renewed interest in order to upgrade it to contemporary standards. The site is surrounded by three streets, and has a steep slope and a 25 metres difference in quota. It was decided to take an unusual approach by separating the various functions that relate to different activities and production needs in order to define a complex of operational units that can work simultaneously and in a standardised manner, according to necessity. The building [Umur Matbaa GOSB] is constructed in reinforced concrete, while the large openings are built with steel frames and brightly coloured glass panels. The complete layout was designed to optimise all productive stages during the industrial printing process, combining technological upgrading with architectural design in a single project.

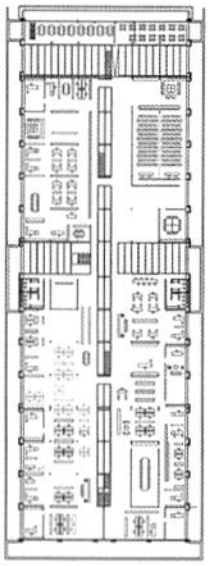

architects
NSMH

type
industrial building

construction
2008

68. Yeşilvadi Mosque

Fatih Sultan Mehmet Cd.
34771 Ümraniye, Istanbul

open to the public

11H, 13Y, 20Ü, C307, Ümraniye Devlet >
HastanYeşilvadi Sapağı

The Yeşilvadi Mosque [Yeşilvadi Camii] is located on the Asian side of the city in the Ümraniye district, on a site that posed certain construction problems because of its proximity to the O-2 ring road. The architects of the Adnan Kazmaoğlu Mimarlık Araştırma Merkezi team designed the new mosque in answer to the urban planning development foreseen for this area of Istanbul. The concept is a combination of contemporary and traditional construction, based on the precepts of historic Ottoman mosque design. This was a quarter with few amenities for the local population, so the new mosque, opened in 2004, provided a large number of services, as well as its role as a place of worship. It embodies the traditional role of the mosque with its ability to become a strategic social gathering centre for the local population. For this reason, as well as the prayer room, the building also includes a library, multifunction spaces, a courtyard, and an open square for public use. Concrete was used according to mosque tradition for the modelling of the large dome, 25 metres in diameter, over the prayer room, which resembles a shell perforated with openings that shed light into the zone dedicated to prayer. Separated from the main mosque building, the cylindrical minaret was designed according to golden ratio proportions, as was the entire mosque structure.

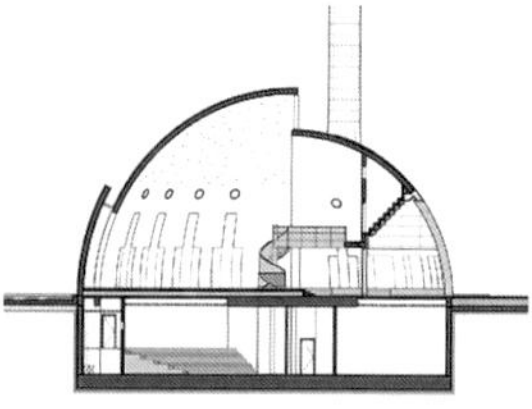

architects
Adnan Kazmaoğlu Mimarlık
Araştırma Merkezi

type
mosque

construction
2004

69. Sur Yapi Offices

Tantavi, Estergon Cd. No:20
34764 Ümraniye, Istanbul

external viewing only

10, 11A, 14YK, 15BK, 15TK, 20, D26, D28 >
Egemenlik Caddesi

The Sur Yapi sales office building [Exen Satis Ofisi] is situated on a hill on the Asian side of Istanbul. It was designed by Tago Architects and built in 2010. The complex is rectangular in shape and covers a surface area of 2,182 square metres spread over three floors housing business and sales offices and exhibition spaces. The south facade is composed of glazed walls and steel walkways that run the length of the building. A clever system of wooden panel shutters protects the interior from the sun; as well as their functional aspect, the panels enhance and underline the design and composition of the facade. The other facades feature large irregular openings that allow glimpses of the interior decor. The combination of glass, wood, and natural stone materials have helped define the personality of the building and its integration in the surrounding landscape.

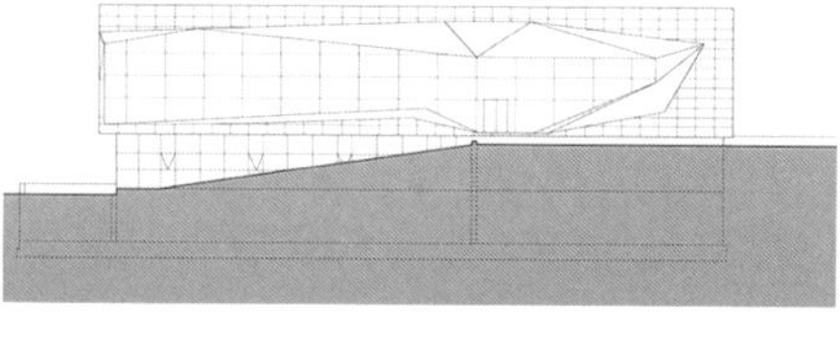

architects
Tago Architects

type
offices

construction
2010

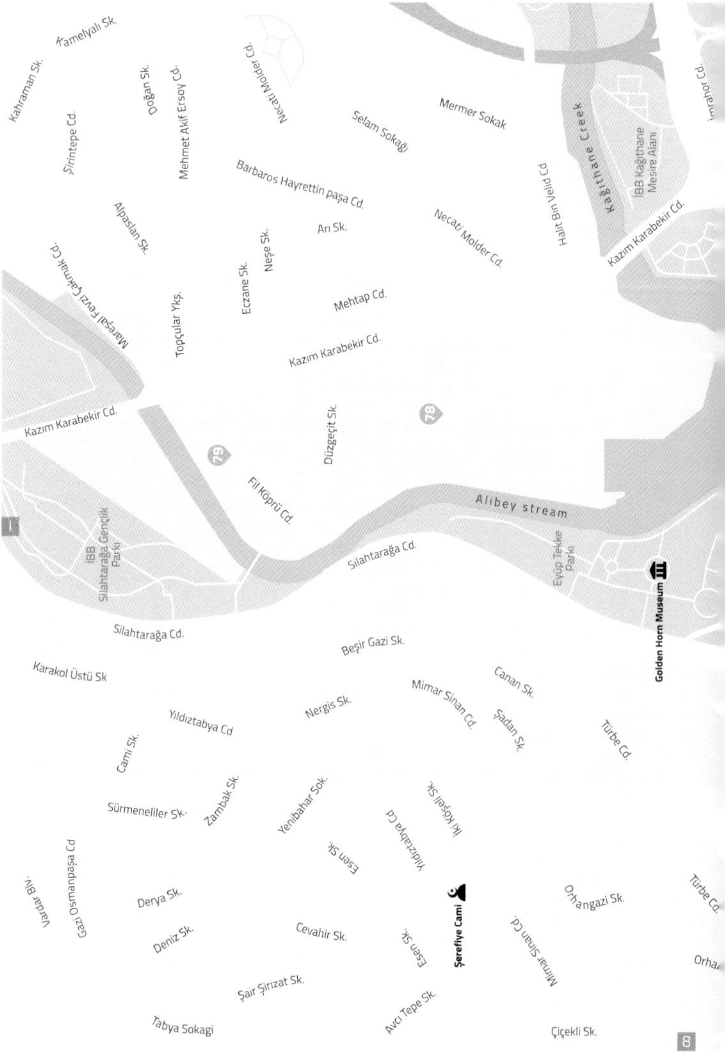
Kamelyalı Sk.
Kahraman Sk.
Doğan Sk.
Mehmet Akif Ersoy Cd.
Necati Molder Cd.
Şirintepe Cd.
Mermer Sokak
Selam Sokağı
Barbaros Hayrettin paşa Cd.
Kağıthane Creek
İBB Kağıthane Mesire Alanı
Halit Bin Velid Cd
Alpaslan Sk.
Arı Sk.
Necati Molder Cd.
Kazım Karabekir Cd.
Mareşal Fevzi Çakmak Cd.
Neşe Sk.
Eczane Sk.
Topçular Ykş.
Mehtap Cd.
Kazım Karabekir Cd.
78
Kazım Karabekir Cd.
Düzgeçit Sk.
79
Fil Köprü Cd.
Alibey stream
I
İBB Silahtarağa Gençlik Parkı
Silahtarağa Cd.
Eyüp Tekke Parkı
Golden Horn Museum
Silahtarağa Cd.
Beşir Gazi Sk.
Karakol Üstü Sk
Canan Sk.
Mimar Sinan Cd.
Nergis Sk.
Yıldıztabya Cd
Şadan Sk.
Türbe Cd.
Cami Sk.
Zambak Sk.
Yenibahar Sok.
İki köşeli Sk.
Sürmeneliler Sk.
Yıldıztabya Cd
Esen Sk.
Gazi Osmanpaşa Cd
Vardar Blv.
Derya Sk.
Şerefiye Cami
Orhangazi Sk.
Türbe Cd.
Deniz Sk.
Cevahir Sk.
Esen Sk.
Mimar Sinan Cd.
Şair Şirinzat Sk.
Avcı Tepe Sk.
Tabya Sokagi
Çiçekli Sk.
8

Kağıthane - Beşiktaş - Sarıyer - Eyüp

70. Fatih Sultan Mehmet Bridge
71. The Seed
72. Yavuz Sultan Selim Bridge
73. Göktürk Arketip Housing
74. Istanbul Grand Airport
75. Sancaklar Mosque
76. Tema Istanbul Showroom
77. Eyüpsultan Kültür Sanat Merkezi
78. SantralIstanbul
79. Studio Santral
80. Nef Primary School
81. Istanbul Sapphire

70. Fatih Sultan Mehmet Bridge

Anadolu Hisarı
34000 Beykoz, Istanbul

open to the public

C300 > Körfez
11H, 15, 15A, 15F, 15KÇ, 15P, 15T, 15ŞN, 121A, C300, D24 > Dolaybağı
22, 22RE, 29D, 40, 40T > Necipbey Bağı

Built between 1986 and 1988 by Freeman Fox & Partners, the "Second Bosphorus bridge" bears the name of Mehmed the Conqueror, the Ottoman Sultan who took Constantinople following the fall of the Byzantine Empire (1453). The Fatih Sultan Mehmet bridge [Fatih Sultan Mehmet Köprüsü] connects the European and Asian districts of Hisarüstü and Kavacık, and is one of the three bridges that currently connect Europe and Asia. It was the second bridge to be built; the first was the 15 Temmuz Şehitler Bridge, opened in 1973, while the most recent is the Yavuz Sultan Selim Bridge, inaugurated in 2016. The bridge is 1,5 kilometres long with a deck width of 39 metres, and is suspended from two steel pylons 175 metres tall. Vertical steel cables support the bridge deck at a quota of 64 metres above sea level. The bridge has eight lanes, with traffic flow in both directions, and carries the Asian Highway 1, Asian Highway 5, and the Istanbul external ring road, Otoyol 2 highway.

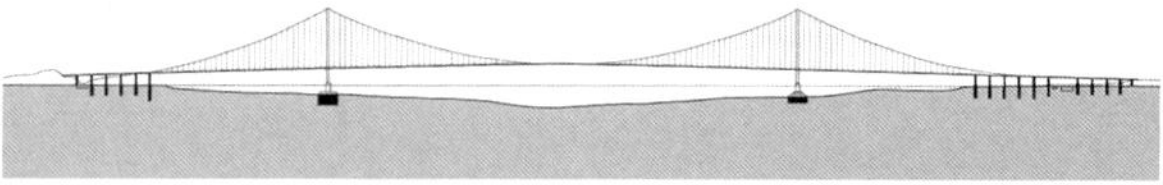

architects
Freeman Fox & Partners

type
infrastructure

construction
1988

71. The Seed

Emirgan Mahallesi,
Sakıp Sabancı Cd. No:42
34467 Sarıyer, Istanbul

open to the public
+90 212 3236050
theseed@gl-events.com
www.theseed.com.tr

22, 22RE, 25E, 40, 40T, 42T, 59RH, EL2 > Çınaraltı

Bebek-Emirgan, Boğaz Hattı, Rumeli Kavağı-Eminönü, Çengelköy-İstinye > Emirgan

Defined as a "Multifunctional concert hall", this project by architecture office NSMH was designed to act in synergy with the activities of the nearby Sakip Sabanci Museum in Emirgan (Sarıyer district). In contrast with the severe straight lines of the structures that enclose it, the concert hall is contained inside a cavity (the seed) constructed in curved steel panels painted externally in vibrant yellow. Part of the "seed" is embedded into the side of the sloping terrain. The hall can seat 330 spectators and has been designed for concerts, conferences and congresses. The building was constructed on a steep slope, so certain parts of the new structure were carved out of the terrain to create two spacious terraced areas. The first outdoor space forms a large balconied terrace at the same height as the floor above the entrance lobby, while the second terraced area, higher up, forms a rooftop garden, on a level with the uppermost part of the slope. The structure that encloses "the seed" is a strong shell built in reinforced concrete for the underground sections, with a lighter steel framework above ground. The exterior of the new construction is faced with stone-filled gabions, making the building almost disappear, and concealing it among the dense trees on the slopes overlooking the Bosphorus.

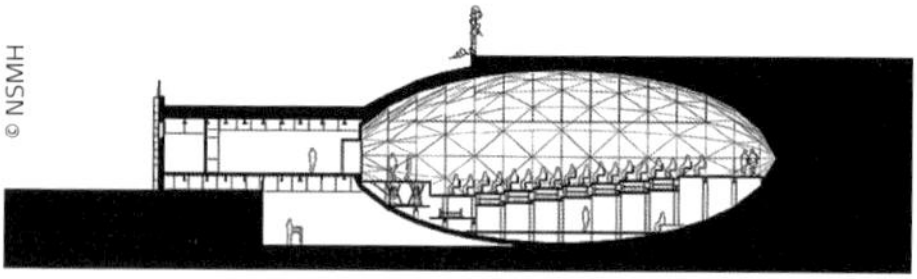

© NSMH

architects
NSMH

type
cultural centre

construction
2009

72. Yavuz Sultan Selim Bridge

Poyraz
34829 Beykoz, Istanbul

open to the public

40, 150 > Köprü Yolu
135 > Yavuz Sultan Selim Köprü Şantiyesi

Slender, dynamic, contemporary. This is the initial impression of the Yavuz Sultan Selim bridge [Yavuz Sultan Selim Köprüsü] located to the north of Istanbul. It is the third bridge over the Bosphorus linking Europe and Asia. The infrastructure designed by engineers, Jean-François Klein and Michel Virlogeux, and constructed by the Italian consortium, Astaldi (now Astaris), in 2016, is a suspended cable-stayed structure, 2,164 metres long. The pillars to which the cables are attached are over 300 metres tall and the main span measures 1,408 metres. It is a record-breaking bridge: it is the longest in the world, with 8 vehicle lanes and two railway lines which link the city with the Sabiha Gökçen and Istanbul Havalimanı airports. The Yavuz Sultan Selim bridge is one of the contemporary architectural designs that has most contributed to the modernisation process in Istanbul, facilitating the links between the two continents to a substantial extent, allowing a large part of the population to move easily and rapidly.

architects
Jean-François Klein,
Michel Virlogeux, Astaldi

type
infrastructure

construction
2016

73. Göktürk Arketip Housing

Göktürk Merkez,
Palmiye Sk No:6
34077 Eyüpsultan, Istanbul

partially open to the public

www.kelesogluholding.com/projeler/arketip-evler

48, 48A, 48D, 48E, 48G, 48K, 48KA, 48L, 48P, 48Y, 50G, AVR3K, B35, H-2 > Hisar Eğitim Okulları

The Arketip Housing Project [Göktürk Arketip Konutları], is a housing project designed by EAA – Emre Arolat Architecture, that was built in the Göktürk area. The local landscape, especially the forest near the southern end of the building, and the investor's decision to build apartments in the area, were the main influences for the architectural design choices. The project is composed of a complex of linear buildings surrounded by a series of common spaces and private gardens. The structure follows a rigorous layout to create a balance between public and private spaces, even inside the individual blocks, where there are shared common areas: corridors, service areas, wet zones and terraces. The facades are composed of a combination of two main materials: stone for the lower porticos and folding wooden shutters on the upper floors. The wooden panels shield the windows of all apartments. The choice of these materials was fundamental for the project since wood and stone integrate perfectly with the surrounding landscape.

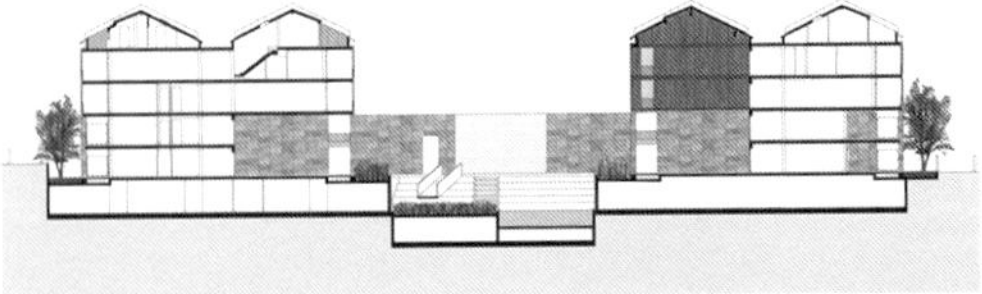

© EAA – Emre Arolat Architecture

© Cemal Emden

architects
EAA – Emre Arolat Architecture

type
residential complex

construction
2010

74. Istanbul Grand Airport

Tayakadın Mahallesi,
Terminal Caddesi No:1
34283 Arnavutköy, Istanbul

open to the public

www.igairport.aero/en

M11 > İstanbul Havalimanı, Kargo Terminali

HVIST-15, HVIST-13, HVIST-8, HVIST-7, H-1, H-2, H-3, H-6, H-8 > İstanbul Havalimanı

The new Istanbul airport [İstanbul Havalimanı], located on the southern coast of the Black Sea, was designed by the London architectural firm, Grimshaw. The new gateway to Turkey is one of the largest airports in the world. The architectural design was inspired by, and integrates, the rich cultural influences and architecture of the historic city in modern style: colour, ornamental motifs, and vaulted ceilings created from micro-perforated panels diffuse daylight, creating a harmonious and luminous atmosphere. The airport is built on two levels. The clear and simple layout generates an easy, dynamic traffic flow for travellers, an essential aspect for organisation and mobility in such a large building: the total surface is over 1,400,000 square metres. In front of the airport is a large plaza, and a transportation hub is located right at the entrance, with immediate access from the airport to train, metro and bus transport to the city.

architects
Grimshaw

type
airport

construction
2018

75. Sancaklar Mosque

Karağaç Mah., Sırtköy Çiftliği Mevkii G 84 Bulvarı
34500 Büyükçekmece, Istanbul

open to the public

144B > Günışığı Konakları, Toskana Vadisi

The Sancaklar Mosque [Sancaklar Camii] is one of the most important examples of contemporary mosque architecture in Turkey. With this design, the EAA – Emre Arolat Architecture firm wanted to focus in concrete terms on formal research into sacred spaces, moving away from all traditional elements to concentrate on the essence of religious space. The building is set in a dip at the bottom of a sloping landscape and blends completely with the natural surroundings through the use of stone and the graduated grass-covered roof, that visually follows the line of the hillside. It is a constant play of contrast between the man-made and the natural. This tension continues within the mosque where the use of raw materials and filtered light from above give the effect of a cave-like space. The Sancaklar mosque is a private, primitive space, focussed on placing man in contact with his soul and with God.

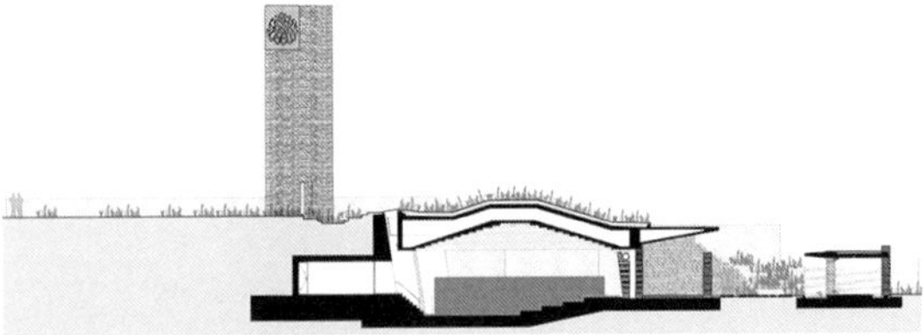

architects
EAA – Emre Arolat Architecture

type
mosque

construction
2012

76. Tema Istanbul Showroom

Atakent, 03 Güney Yanyolu
34307 Küçükçekmece, Istanbul

Mon - Sat / 9 am - 6 pm
+90 212 9700000
info@temaistanbul.com
www.temaistanbul.com

78G, 78Ş, 89YB, 98AB, 141K, AVR1, MR50, MR52 > Köprü
78G, 78Ş, AVR1, MR50 > Sultan Alparslan İlkokulu

The showroom is composed of three parallelepipeds with reflective glass facades enclosed within a white elliptical steel ribbed structure. It is surrounded by green lawns, and is suspended above an artificial reflecting pool. The Tema Istanbul Showroom appears as a floating structure to visitors as they walk along the wooden bridge leading to the entrance. The building is divided into three floors, each assigned to different functions: sales offices, bank offices, apartment model display and gallery space. Yazgan Design Architecture designed the interior as an experiment on perceived depth of space. This was achieved using green surfaces, led lighting, skylights and glass walls. The strategy not only expands the perceived space but helps create a relationship between the surrounding landscape and the interior, so that the building becomes part of a whole.

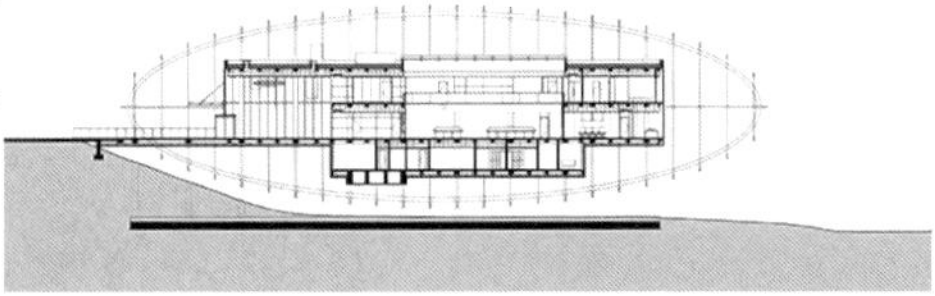

architects
Yazgan Design Architecture

type
showroom

construction
2013

77. Eyüpsultan Kültür Sanat Merkezi

Merkez, Silahtarağa Cd. No:18
34050 Eyüpsultan, Istanbul

open to the public
+90 212 4400584
kultur@eyupsultan.bel.tr
kultursanat.eyupsultan.bel.tr

36CE, 37M, 39, 39A, 39B, 39D, 39K, 39O, 39Y, 39Ç, 41Y, 44B, 48A, 48E, 50B, 50K, 50V, 50Y, 94Y, 99, 99Y, 399B, 399C, A27, A34, A40, B35 > Çeltik

The Eyüp Cultural Centre [Eyüpsultan Kültür Sanat Merkezi], represents a completely new concept in the panorama of Turkish architecture for its spatial and functional quality. The Centre was designed by EAA – Emre Arolat Architecture in 2013, and is situated on the north-western shore of the Golden Horn. The structure is perfectly integrated in the landscape and counterbalances the difference in height between street level and the shore by creating a connecting element. The roof of the Centre acts as a walkway ramp to provide pedestrians with easy access to the Haliç beach. Thanks to the continuous glass walls, the public using the walkway has a clear view of all activities being held inside the building. The functional concept of the roof-ramp and the transparent structure are the two fundamental elements that represent the open welcoming nature of this centre, designed to create a connection with the public in spatial, cultural and visual domains.

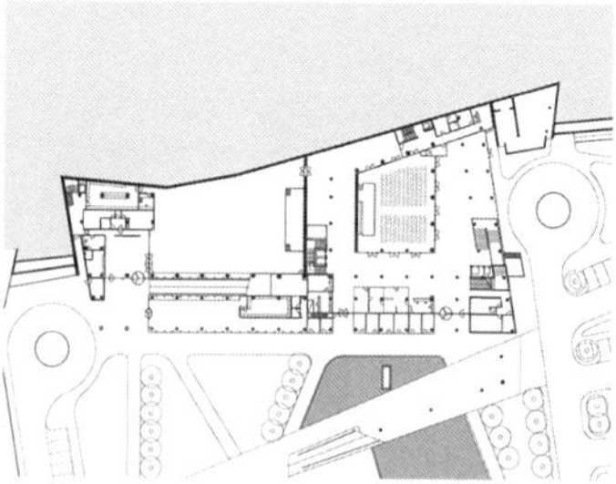

© EAA – Emre Arolat Architecture

architects
EAA – Emre Arolat Architecture

type
cultural centre

construction
2013

78. Santralİstanbul

Eski Silahtarağa Elektrik Santrali, Kazım Karabekir Cad. No:2
34060 Eyüpsultan, Istanbul

Mon - Sun / 9 am - 5.30 pm
+90 212 3117878
info@santralistanbul.org
www.santralistanbul.org

50E, 38M, 49, 49B, 50D, 37T, 36T, 49T, 55B, 41Y, 49GB, 49G, 38G, 50T, 44B, 47, 50S, 47E >
Bilgi Üniversitesi

Santralİstanbul is a redevelopment project underway in one of the most deteriorated and neglected areas in the city. This project, aimed at creating a museum and educational centre, was realised between 2004 and 2007 by the team of architects, EAA – Emre Arolat Architecture and NSMH. The site of the former Ottoman Empire power plant is a complex of buildings that now forms the campus, and the Energy Museum, designed as an independent structure built of steel beams and glass to preserve its original industrial character. The complex also includes the Main Gallery, a space for contemporary art exhibitions. The structure was designed as a large steel mesh parallelepiped, placed on a stone base. During the day, the building appears heavy and solid, but changes completely at night, when it is transformed, to become an enormous glowing lantern. The internal lighting displays the building's structure and connection system. The composition of the different buildings provides a continuous dialogue between modernity and tradition, encapsulating the personality and character of Istanbul.

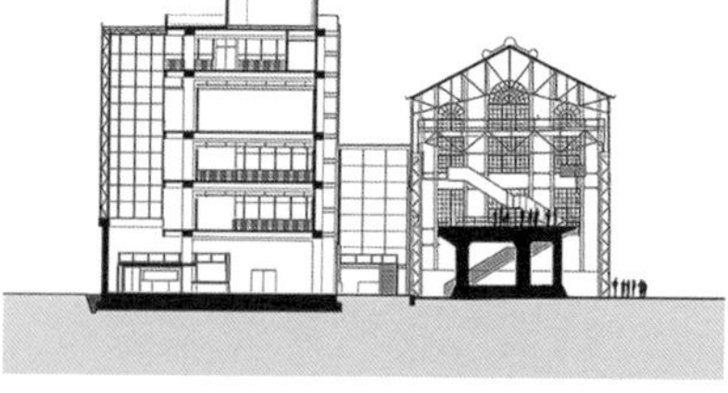

© EAA – Emre Arolat Architecture

© Cemal Emden

architects
EAA – Emre Arolat
Architecture, NSMH

type
museum, university

construction
2007

79. Studio Santral

Fil Köprü Cd. No:4
34060 Eyüpsultan, Istanbul

partially open to the public
+90 533 4858656
info@studiosantral.com
studiosantral.com

36T, 37T, 38G, 38KT, 38M, 38T, 41Y, 44B, 47, 47A, 47E, 47K, 47N, 47Ç, 49, 49A, 49B, 49G, 49GB, 49K, 49M, 49T, 49Y, 49Z, 50D, 50E, 50L, 50N, 50S, 55B, 55Y, 399B, A49, AVR2, AVR3K, B44, Şişhane - Vialand, Şişli - Vialand
> Silahtar

T5 > Üniversite

The new Studio Santral residential building for students in the Bilgi Silahtarağa University Campus in the Eyüp district, was designed by the Erginoğlu & Çalışlar Mimarlık firm, with architectural references to the 1st National Architecture Period in Turkey. The shape of the site dictated the narrow rectangular structure, 150 metres long. It was slotted into the section of the site between the existing buildings and Fil Köprüsü Avenue and creates a continuous balance between its roles as a barrier and a filter between the city and the campus. The single narrow rectangular block is divided into different sections by repeated voids and spaces that contain loggias and terrace gardens. These interruptions in the long block give the impression of four distinct units and form an enclosure that is also open and accessible to the city. The steel framework bearing structure is designed to adapt to each modular residential unit. The module types vary according to different requirements and the combination of layout variations are visible on the facade through the regular pattern of the window openings that provide an assymetrical rhythm through the dynamic colours of the window framings.

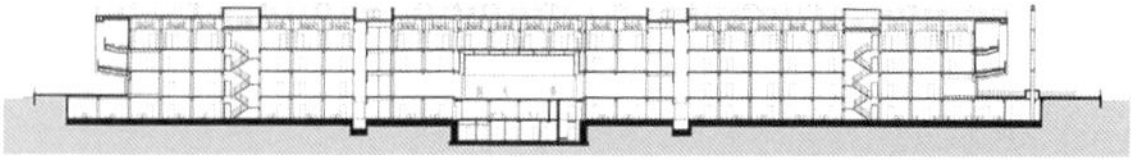

architects
Erginoğlu & Çalışlar Mimarlık

type
dormitory

construction
2014

80. Nef Primary School

Ortabayır, Gürhan Sk. No:13
34413 Kağıthane, Istanbul

partially open to the public
+90 212 2640882

nefilkokulu.meb.k12.tr

B33, Başak Konutları-Beşiktaş, Şişli-Yahya Kemal > Gürhan Sokak

In 2014, the team of architects from Çinici Mimarlık was asked to work on a project for a kindergarten and primary school complex. The site is adjacent to the renowned Büyükdere Avenue financial district, and is an area which has been a subject of debate concerning its "urban regeneration" since 2000. The school complex has an overall surface of 7,284 square metres and is located close to the local mosque. The link between the scholastic and religious buildings has inspired the concept that the complex could form a cultural and social centre for the whole neighbourhood, located in the Kağıthane district. The project is constructed around the school courtyard, the true spacial hub of the intervention. The main structure is composed of three separate, but connected, buildings: a long classroom block, a building housing the administration offices, located adjacent to the mosque, and finally, a double-height hall for indoor sports activities. The library is positioned on the ground floor below the classroom block, and receives direct daylight from the enclosed garden area of the kindergarten. The three blocks are built in reinforced concrete, left exposed inside the buildings, and rendered with a white plaster finish on the external walls.

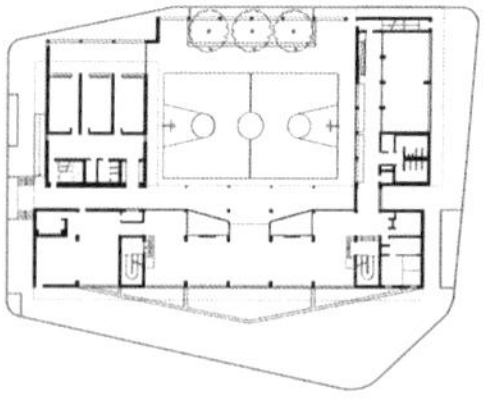

© Çinici Mimarlık

architects
Çinici Mimarlık

type
school

construction
2014

81. Istanbul Sapphire

Emniyetevleri,
Eski Büyükdere Cd. No:1
34415 Kağıthane, Istanbul

Mon - Sun / 10 am - 10 pm
+90 212 2688080
bilhi@istanbulsapphire.com
www.sapphireavym.com

M2 > Levent

41, 41A > Levent Metro

The Istanbul Sapphire skyscraper, designed and built in 2011 by Tabanlioğlu Architects, is the tallest building in Turkey. It is located in the "business administration" area of the city and contains residential apartments, a shopping centre, and leisure activities like a swimming pool and common areas with panoramic views of Istanbul. The high-rise building has an innovative design; it is composed of two glass facades that curve outwards at the base to form the roof of the shopping centre structure on the ground floor. This element forms both facade and roof at the same time. The main structure of the building is composed of two separate shells divided by a vertical corridor that houses gardens and terraces for the apartments, terminating in a covered roof terrace with restaurant. The elegant transparent design has opened up a way for new architectural concepts in the administration area of Istanbul.

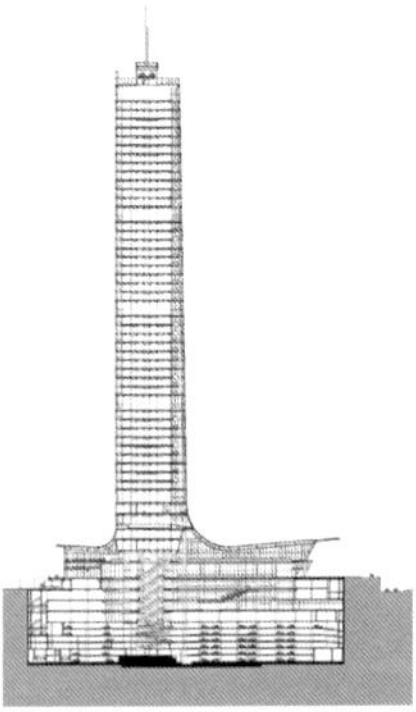

© Tabanlioğlu Architects

architects
Tabanlıoğlu Architects

type
commercial centre,
residential building

construction
2010

Museums

Büyük Saray Mozaikleri Müzesi
Mosaic Museum
-
Sultanahmet Mahallaesi Kabasakal Cad. Arasta Çarşısı Sok. No:53, 34122 Fatih, Istanbul

www.muze.gov.tr
ayasofyamuzesi@ktb.gov.tr
Tel +90 (212) 518 18 05

Florya Atatürk Deniz Köşkü
Atatürk Mansion Marine Museum
-
Basınköy, Çekmece İstanbul Cd. No:23, 34153 Bakırköy, Istanbul

www.millisaraylar.gov.tr
iktm34@ktb.gov.tr
Tel +90 (212) 426 51 51

Türk ve İslam Eserleri Müzesi
Turkish and Islamic Arts Museum
-
Binbirdirek, Atmeydanı Cd. No:12, 34122 Fatih, Istanbul

www.muze.gov.tr
Tel +90 (212) 518 18 05

İstanbul Arkeoloji Müzesi
Archaeology Museum
-
Cankurtaran, 34122 Fatih, Istanbul

www.istanbularkeoloji.gov.tr
istanbularkeoloji@ktb.gov.tr
Tel +90 (212) 520 77 41

Küçüksu Kasrı
Küçüksu Palace museum
-
Göksu, Küçüksu Cd. No:12, 34815 Beykoz, Istanbul

www.millisaraylar.gov.tr
info@millisaraylar.gov.tr
Tel +90 (212) 332 33 03

PTT Pul Müzesi
Post Office Museum
-
Hobyar, Büyük Postane Cd. No:44, 34112 Fatih, Istanbul

www.pttpulmuzesi.org.tr
info@ptt.gov.tr
Tel +90 (212) 520 90 37

Saray Koleksiyonları Müzesi
Palace Collections Museum
-
Vişnezade Mah, Dolmabahçe Cd., 34357 Beşiktaş, Istanbul

www.millisaraylar.gov.tr
info@millisaraylar.gov.tr
Tel +90 (212) 236 90 00

Yerebatan Sarnıcı
Archaeology Site
-
Yerebatan Cad. Alemdar Mah. 1/3 34410 Sultanahmet, Fatih, Istanbul

www.yerebatansarnici.com
info@yerebatan.com
Tel +90 (212) 522 12 59

Theatres

Cemal Reșit Rey Concert Hall
Harbiye, Dar'ül Bedayi Cad No:6, 34371 Șișli, Istanbul
www.crrkonsersalonu.ibb.istanbul
Tel +90 (212) 232 98 30

Fatih Reșat Nuri Sahnesi
Atatürk Bulvarı Cemal Yener Tosyalı Cad.No:2-36, Unkapanı Fatih, Istanbul
sehirtiyatrolari.ibb.istanbul
Tel +90 (212) 455 39 00

İBB Șehir Tiyatroları Musahipzade Celâl Sahnesi
Aziz Mahmut Hüdayi, Halk Cd. No:84, 34672 Üsküdar, Istanbul
Tel +90 (212) 553 03 97

Kadıköy Haldun Taner Stage
Caferağa, Rıhtım Cd., 34710 Kadıköy, Istanbul
www.sehirtiyatrolari.ibb.istanbul
Tel +90 (212) 349 04 63

Kadıköy'ün Kültür Beșiği Süreyya Operası
Osmanağa, General Asım Gündüz Cd. No:29, 34714 Kadıköy, Istanbul
www.kadikoy.gov
kadikoy@istanbul.gov.tr
Tel +90 (212) 346 15 31

Kenter Theater
Ergenekon, Halaskargazi Cd. No:9, 34373 Șișli, Istanbul
www.dostlartiyatrosu.com
bilgi@dostlartiyatrosu.com
Tel +90 (212) 246 35 89

Moda Stage Theatre
Osmanağa, Halil Ethem Sokak, General Asım Gündüz Cd., 34714 Kadıköy, Istanbul
www.modasahnesi.com
bilgi@modasahnesi.com
Tel +90 (212) 330 58 00

Șehir Tiyatroları
Harbiye Mahallesi, Darülbedayi Caddesi No:3, Șișli, Istanbul
www.sehirtiyatrolari.ibb.istanbul
tiyatro@ibb.gov.tr
Tel +90 (212) 455 39 00

Zorlu Performing Arts Center
Levazım, Koru Sokağı No:2, 34340 Beșiktaș, Istanbul
www.zorlupsm.com
info@zorlupsm.com
Tel +90 (212) 912 37 76

Restaurants

••• expensive
•• mid-range
• inexpensive

Akdeniz Hatay Sofrası •••
Ahmediye Cad. No: 44/A, Fatih, Istanbul
www.akdenizhataysofrasi.com
Tel +90 (212) 444 7247

Balıkçı Sabahattin •••
Seyit Hasan Kuyu Sok. No:1, 34122 Cankurtaran-Eminönü, Istanbul
www.balikcisabahattin.com
Tel +90 (212) 458 1824

Ciya sofrasi •••
Caferaga Mah. Güneslibahce Sk. 48/B, Kadiköy, Istanbul
www.ciya.com
info@ciya.com.tr
Tel + 90 (216) 330 31 90

Hamdi restaurant • • •
Refik Saydam Cad. No:19, Tepebaşı- Beyoğlu, Istanbul
www.hamdi.com
info@hamdirestorant.com.tr
Tel +90 (212) 377 25 09

Hocapaşa Pidecisi • •
Hoca Paşa, Ankara Caddesi & Hoca Paşa Sokak No:11, 34110 Fatih, Istanbul
www.hocapasa.com
info@hocapasa.com.tr
Tel +90 (212) 512 09 90

Ismet Baba • • •
Kuzguncuk Çarşı Caddesi No:1/A, 34674 Üsküdar, Istanbul
www.ismetbaba.com
info@ismetbaba.com.tr
Tel +90 (212) 553 12 32

Kanaat Lokantası • • •
Selmanipak cad. No:9, Üsküdar, Istanbul
www.kanaatlokantasi.com
Tel +90 (212) 341 54 44

Konyalı Lokantası • • •
Sultanahmet Mahallesi Topkapı Sarayı, 34122 Fatih, Istanbul
www.konyalilokantasi.com
saray@konyalilokantasi.com
Tel +90 (212) 513 96 96

Metet Közde Döner • • •
Kuzguncuk Mh., İnci Çayırlı Sokak (Tufan Sk.) No:2, 34674 Üsküdar, Istanbul
www.metetdoner.com
iletisim@metetdoner.com
Tel +90 (212) 553 33 33

Sanli Mangal • • •
İskenderpaşa mahallesi Ragıpbey caddesi No:29, Fatih Aksaray, Istanbul
info@sanlimangal.com
Tel +90 (212) 635 40 54

Saray Muhallebicisi • • •
Istiklal Cd. No:173, Beyoglu, Istanbul
www.saraymuhallebicisi.com
Tel +90 (212) 292 34 34

Sur Ocakbaşı • • •
Zeyrek Mah Kadınlar Pazarı, İtfaiye Cd. No:19 D:No:19, 34083 Fatih, Istanbul
www.surocakbasi.com
Tel +90 (212) 533 80 88

Tarihi karakoy balikcisi • • •
Tersane Cad, Kürekçiler Kapısı Sk. No:45, 34420 Beyoğlu, Istanbul
www.karakoybalikcisi.com
info@karakoybalikcisi.com
Tel +90 (212) 243 40 80

Tarihi Sultanahmet Köftecisi • • •
Alemdar Mh., Divan Yolu Caddesi, No:12, Istanbul
www.sultanahmetkoftesi.com
info@brasseriezedel.com
Tel +90 (212) 520 05 66

Urfalı Hacı Usta • •
Sofular Mah.Ragıpbey Sk.No:23/B, Aksaray-Fatih, Istanbul
www.urfalihaciusta.com
info@urfalihaciusta.com
Tel +90 (212) 534 99 62

Hotels

• • • expensive
• • mid-range
• inexpensive

AJWA Sultanahmet • • •
Piyerloti No:30, Sultanahmet, Çemberlitaş,
34490 Fatih, Istanbul
www.ajwa.com.tr
info@ajwa.com.tr
Tel +90 (216) 638 22 00

Bankerhan Hotel • •
Bereketzade Mahallesi, Banker Sokak No:2 Beyoglu
Galata, 34420 Beyoglu, Istanbul
www.bankerhanhotel.com
info@bankerhanhotel.com
Tel +90 (216) 243 56 17

City Hall Hotel •
Emin Sinan Mah, Pertev Paşa Sk. No:39,
34126 Fatih, Istanbul
www.cityhallhotelistanbul.com
info@cityhallhotelistanbul.com
Tel +90 (216) 516 60 11

Çırağan Palace Kempinski Istanbul • • •
Çırağan Caddesi 32, 34349 Besiktas,
Istanbul
www.kempinski.com
reservations.ciraganpalace@kempinski.com
Tel +90 (216) 326 46 46

Euro Design Hotel • •
Hobyar Mahallesi, Ankara Caddesi 24,
34110 Fatih, Istanbul
www.eurodesignhotel.com
info@eurodesignhotel.com
Tel +90 (216) 520 56 17

Four Seasons Hotel Istanbul at Sultanahmet • • •
Tevkifhane Sok., No:1, Sultanahmet, 34110 Fatih,
Istanbul
www.fourseasons.com
Tel +90 (216) 402 22 00

Four Seven Hotel •
Aksaray, İnkılap Cd. No:1/1, 34096 Fatih, Istanbul
www.foursevenhotel.com
Tel +90 (216) 588 50 07

Hira Hotel •
İskendepaşa Mah. Oruç Gazi Sok. No:1,
34091 Fatih, Istanbul
www.hirahotel.com
info@hirahotel.com
Tel +90 (216) 438 01 50

Istanroom by Keo •
Cumhuriyet Mah. Ergenekon Cad. No:32,
34379 Sisli, Istanbul
www.istanroom.com
info@istanroom.com
Tel +90 (216) 253 70 70

Mercure Istanbul Altunizade • •
Altunizade Mah. Kısıklı Cad. Oymacı Sokak No:9,
34662 Üsküdar, Istanbul
www.mercureistanbulaltunizade.com
H8973@accor.com
Tel +90 (216) 333 00 00

My Dora Hotel •
Rihtim Cad. Recaizade Sok. No:6, 34716 Kadikoy,
Istanbul
www.mydorahotel.com
dora@mydora.com.tr
Tel +90 (216) 414 83 50

Park Hyatt Istanbul - Macka Palas • •
Tesvikiye, Bronz Sokak No:4, Macka, 34367 Sisli,
Istanbul
www.hyatt.com
istanbul.park@hyatt.com
Tel +90 (216) 315 12 34

Pera Palace Hotel • • •
Mesrutiyet cad. No:52, 34430 Beyoglu, Istanbul
www.perapalace.com
reservations@perapalace.com
Tel +90 (216) 377 40 00

Piya Sport Hotel • •
Mimar Kemalettin Mh. Sekbanbasi Sk. No:2,
34427 Fatih, Istanbul
www.piyasporthotel.com
info@piyasporthotel.com
Tel +90 (216) 458 90 00

Wyndham Grand Istanbul Kalamış Marina Hotel • • •
Fener Kalamis Cad. No:38, 34726 Kadikoy, Istanbul
www.wyndhamhotels.com
Tel +90 (216) 400 00 00

Architectural offices

Adnan Kazmaoğlu Mimarlık Araştırma Merkezi
Vişnezade Acısu Sok. No:9 Arzu, D:Apt. D:5, 34357
Beşiktaş, Istanbul
www.adnankazmaoglu.com
info@adnankazmaoglu.com
Tel +90 (212) 230 77 95

Ahmet Alataş Workshop
İstanbul Caddesi Dere Sok. No:52, 34075
Kemerburgaz-Eyüp, Istanbul
www.ahmetalatas.com
Tel +90 (212) 368 80 70

Aytaç Architects
Taş Mektep Sok. No:51/1 Erenköy, Kadıköy, Istanbul
www.aytacarchitects.com
info@aytacarchitects.com
Tel +90 (216) 369 29 29

Cafer Bozkurt Architecture
Arnavutköy Dere Sok. 44, 34345 Beşiktaş, Istanbul
www.cba-ist.com
info@cba-ist.com
Tel +90 (212) 265 75 91

Çinici Mimarlık
Salacak İskele Arkası Sokağı, 34668 Üsküdar,
Istanbul
www.cinicimimarlik.com
m.info@cinicimimarlik.com
Tel +90 (216) 343 98 87

CM Mimarlık
Nişantaşı Ihlamur Yolu Sk. 69-53, Teşvikiye,
34365 Şişli, Istanbul
www.cmmimarlik.com
info@cmmimarlik.com.tr
Tel +90 (212) 232 62 97

DB Architects
Atabey Sok. No:8 Hasanpaşa, Kadıköy, Istanbul
www.dbarchitects.com.tr
info@dbarchitects.com.tr
Tel +90 (212) 545 50 17

DİLEKCİ Architects (DDA)
Mahmut Cavuş Sokak No: 15, 34460 Istinye, Istanbul
www.dilekci.com
info@dilekci.com
Tel +90 (212) 277 11 50

EAA – Emre Arolat Architecture
Levent, Nispetiye Mah., Aytar Cad. No:24 Kat:3-4,
34340 Istanbul
www.emrearolat.com
info@emrearolat.com
Tel +90 (212) 284 70 73

Erginoğlu & Çalışlar Mimarlık
Ortaköy, Şair Necati Sk. No:16, 34347 Beşiktaş,
Istanbul
www.ecarch.com
ecmim@ecarch.com
Tel +90 (212) 310 82 75

Ergün Mimarlık
Fenerbahçe, Hacı Mehmet Sk. No:24, 34726
Kadıköy/Istanbul
www.ergunmimarlik.com
info@ergunmimarlik.com.tr
Tel +90 (216) 360 00 51

GAD Architecture
Abdi Ipekci Cad. Park Apt. No:19-1
Kat: 6, 34367 Istanbul
www.gadarchitecture.com
info(at)gadarchitecture.com
Tel +90 (212) 327 51 25

GMW Mimarlık
Vişnezade, Süleyman Seba Caddesi BJK Plaza
No:48 A Blok Daire:123 34357 Beşiktaş, Istanbul
www.gmwmimarlik.com
info@gmwmimarlik.com
Tel +90 (212) 327 19 40

MArS-Architects
Hoca Ali Sokak 8/A, 34425 Galata, Istanbul
www.mars-architects.com
mars@mars-architects.com
Tel +90 (212) 243 59 80

Mimarlar ve Han Tümertekin
Çınarlı Çeşme Sokağı, 34345 Beşiktaş, Istanbul
www.mimarlar.com
mimarlar@mimarlar.com
Tel +90 (212) 259 47 36

NSMH
Kuzguncuk, Bostan Sk. 11/A, 34674 Üsküdar, Istanbul
www.nsmh.com
bilgi@nsmh.co
Tel +90 (216) 310 08 70

Salon Alper Derinboğaz
Gümüşsuyu Mah. İndigo Apt. 41/7 7th Floor, Beyoğlu, Istanbul
www.salonarchitects.com
hello@salonarchitects.com
Tel +90 (212) 328 25 50

ŞANALarc
Arnavutköy, Abdülhak Molla Sk. No:19, 34345 Beşiktaş, Istanbul
www.sanalarc.com
is@sanalarc.com
Tel +90 (212) 358 02 04

Saruhan Mimarlık
Ahmet Yesevi, Anadoluhisarı, Sine Sk. No:22, 34810 Beykoz, Istanbul
www.saruhanmimarlik.com
saruhan@saruhanmimarlik.com
Tel +90 (212) 308 49 56

Sinan Genim
Kuleli Caddesi, Uzumozu Sokak No:5, Cengelkoy, 34684 Üsküdar, Istanbul
www.sinangenim.com
sinan@sinangenim.com
Tel +90 (212) 321 26 64

Studio Vertebra
Kısıklı Cad. No:28 Kat:-1 Altunizade, 34662 Üsküdar, Istanbul
www.studiovertebra.com
info@studiovertebra.com
Tel +90 (216) 550 39 68

Superpool
Büyük Parmakkapı Sokak 14/4, 34433 Beyoğlu, Istanbul
www.superpool.org
office@superpool.org
Tel +90 (212) 252 74 24

Suyabatmaz Demirel Architects
Asmalı Mescit, Orhan Adlı Apaydın Sk. No:21, 34430 Beyoğlu, Istanbul
www.9-4architects.com
istanbul@19-4architects.com
Tel +90 (212) 265 07 01

Tabanlıoğlu Architects
Passage Petits-Champs Mesrutiyet Caddesi No:67, 34430 Beyoğlu, Istanbul
www.tabanlioglu.com
info@tabanlioglu.com
Tel +90 (212) 251 21 11

Tago Architects
Kısıklı Caddesi No:4 Sarkuysan-ak İş Merkezi, Altunizade, 34662 Istanbul
www.tagomimarlik.com
istanbul@tagoarchitects.com
Tel +90 (216) 651 77 77

Teğet
Sadi Konuralp Caddesi Nejat Eczacıbaşı Binası, No:5 K:3, 34430 Şişhane, Istanbul
www.teget.com
info@teget.com
Tel +90 (212) 343 34 85

Yapı Merkezi
Burhaniye Mh. Haji Rashid Pasha Street No:4, 34676 Üsküdar, Istanbul
www.yapimerkezi.com
yminfo@ym.com.tr
Tel +90 (216) 321 90 00

Index by architect

Index by project

Kargo Terminali
İstanbul Havalimanı (Airport)
M11
İhsaniye
Göktürk
Kemerburgaz
Hasdal
Kağıthane
Gayrettepe
Hacıosman
Darüşşafaka
Atatürk Oto Sanayi
İTÜ Ayazağa
Sanayi
Seyrantepe
Vadistanbul
F3
M2
4.Levent
Levent
Etiler
Nispetiye
M6
Gayrettepe
Zincirlikuyu
Mecidiyeköy
Şişli Mecidiye
Çağlayan
Okmeydanı Hastane
Fulya
Yıldız
Osmanbey
Darülaceze PERPA
Taşkışla
Maçka
Okmeydanı
Taksim
Kayaşehir Merkez
Toplu Konutlar
M3
Şehir Hastanesi
Onurkent
Başakşehir Metrokent
Başak Konutları
Siteler
Turgut Özal
İkitelli Sanayi
Ziya Gökalp Mahallesi
Olimpiyat
M9
B2
Bahçeşehir
T4
Mescid-i Selam
Cebeci
Sultançiftliği
Yenimahalle
Hacı Şükrü
50.Yıl Baştabya
Cumhuriyet Mah.
Tekstilkent Giyimkent
KİPTAŞ Venezia
Kazım Karabekir
Yeşilpınar
Veysel Karani Akşemsettin
Çırçır Mah.
Alibeyköy Cep Otogarı
Alibeyköy Metro
Nurtepe
Alibeyköy
Alibeyköy Merk.
Üniversite
Silahtarağa Mahallesi
Eyüpsultan Devlet Hastanesi
Eyüpsultan Teleferik
Piyer Loti
Eyüp
Feshane
Halıcıoğlu
Ayvansaray
Ayvansaray Eyüpsultan
Balat
Fener
Cibali
Küçükpazar
Haliç
Beyoğlu
Şişhane Zemin İst.
Eminönü
Sirkeci
Gülhane
MASKO
Oruç Reis
Karadeniz Mah.
Yenimahalle
Karadeniz
İSTOÇ
M7
Bahariye
Bölge Parkı
Göztepe Mah.
Mahmutbey
Taşköprü
Ali Fuat Başgil
Bosna Çukurçeşme
Sağmalcılar
Atatürk Mah.
Esenyurt Meydan
Yenimahalle
Kirazlı Bağcılar
Bağcılar Meydan
Üçyüzlü
Menderes
Esenler
Uluyol-Bereç
Rami
Topçular
Demirkapı
Şehitlik
Edirnekapı
Otogar
Kocatepe
Bağcılar
T1
M1B
Güneştepe
Yavuz Selim
Soğanlı
Akıncılar
Güngören
Terazidere
Davutpaşa YTÜ
Merter
Sağmalcılar
Bayrampaşa Maltepe
Vatan
Topkapı-Ulubatlı
Emniyet-Fatih
Aksaray
Haseki
Yusufpaşa
Laleli İstanbul Ü.
Vezneciler İst. Ü.
Beyazıt Kapalıçarşı (Grand Bazaar)
Çemberlitaş (Burnt Column)
Yenikapı
M1A
M1B
M2
Beylikdüzü Sondurak
Beykent
Cumhuriyet Mahallesi
Beylikdüzü
Güzelyurt
Haramidere Sanayi
Beylikdüzü Belediye
Haramidere
Saadetdere Mahallesi
Mustafa Kemal Paşa
Cihangir Üniversite Mah.
B1
B2
Halkalı
Avcılar Merk. Ü. Kampüsü
Şükrübey
Mustafa Kemal
İBB Sos. Tes.
K.Çekmece
Cennet Mah.
Florya
Beşyol
Sefaköy
Florya Akvaryum
Yeşilköy
Yeşilyurt
Ataköy
Merter Teks.Merk.
Mehmet Akif
Zeytinburnu
Bakırköy İncirli
Ataköy Şirinevler
Yenibosna
DTM-İstanbul Fuar Merkezi
Atatürk Havalimanı (Airport)
Bahçelievler
Bakırköy
Bakırköy-İDO
Mithatpaşa
Seyitnizam Akşemsettin
Merkezefendi
Topkapı Şehit M. Cambaz
C.Bağ
Cevizlibağ AÖY
Topkapı
Pazartekke
Çapa Şehremini
Fındıkzade
Fetihkapı
Zeytinburnu
Kazlıçeşme
T6
Yenimahalle

- **M1A** Yenikapı-Atatürk Havalimanı Metro Hattı
  Metro Line
- **M1B** Yenikapı-Kirazlı Metro Hattı
  Metro Line
- **M2** Yenikapı-Seyrantepe-Hacıosman Metro Hattı
  Metro Line
- **M3** Kirazlı-Kayaşehir Merkez Metro Hattı
  Metro Line
- **M4** Kadıköy-Sabiha Gökçen Havalimanı Metro Hattı
  Metro Line
- **M5** Üsküdar-Çekmeköy Metro Hattı
  Metro Line
- **M6** Levent-Boğaziçi Ü./Hisarüstü Metro Hattı
  Metro Line
- **M7** Yıldız-Mahmutbey Metro Hattı
  Metro Line
- **M8** Bostancı-Parseller Metro Hattı
  Metro Line
- **M9** Bahariye-Olimpiyat Metro Hattı
  Metro Line
- **M11** Gayrettepe-İstanbul Havalimanı Metro Hattı (TCDD)
  Metro Line
- **TF1** Maçka-Taşkışla Teleferik Hattı
  Cable Car
- **TF2** Eyüp-Piyer Loti Teleferik Hattı
  Cable Car
- **T1** Kabataş-Bağcılar Tramvay Hattı
  Tram Line
- **T2** Taksim-Tünel Nostaljik Tramvay (İETT)
  Heritage Tram
- **T3** Kadıköy-Moda Tramvay Hattı
  Tram Line
- **T4** Topkapı-Mescid-i Selam Tramvay Hattı
  Tram Line
- **T5** Eminönü-Alibeyköy Tramvay Hattı
  Tram Line
- **F1** Taksim-Kabataş Füniküler Hattı
  Funicular Line
- **F2** Karaköy-Beyoğlu Tarihi Tünel (İETT)
  Tunnel (Heritage Funicular)
- **F3** Seyrantepe-Vadistanbul Füniküler Hattı
  Funicular Line
- **F4** Boğaziçi Ü./Hisarüstü-Aşiyan Füniküler Hattı
  Funicular Line
- **B1** Halkalı-Gebze Banliyö Hattı (Marmaray-TCDD)
  Suburban Line
- **B2** Halkalı-Bahçeşehir Banliyö Hattı (TCDD)
  Suburban Line
- Metrobüs Hattı (İETT)
  Bus Rapid Transit

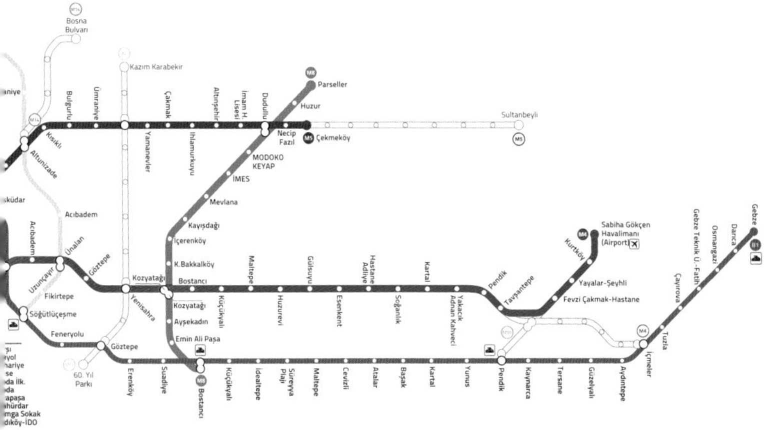

This volume was printed in May 2024
by ABC Tipografia, Calenzano, Florence